M

meet b

meet bathsheba

dramatic portraits
of biblical women

ROSANNE GARTNER

Judson Press

Valley Forge

Library of Congress Cataloging-in-Publication Data
Gartner, Rosanne.
    Meet Bathsheba: dramatic portraits of biblical women. / Rosanne Gartner.
       p.   cm.
    ISBN 0-8170-1355-5 (pbk.)
      1. Women in the Bible.   2. Women in the Bible—Drama.   3. Monologue.
I. Title.
BS575.G37   2000
220.9'2'082—dc21   99-058737

Printed in the U.S.A.

06 05 04 03 02 01 00

10 9 8 7 6 5 4 3 2 1

Contents

Preface

There are countless women in the Bible, many of whom are lost in obscurity. Many are not even named. Even those whose names are familiar are often lost in the text. But each one plays an important role in the plan God has for his people.

The Lord has blessed me with a desire to really know the women of the Bible. I also enjoy the challenge of research. Putting the two together can lead to some very exciting things.

Being given an opportunity to lead an adult Sunday school class is always delightful, although challenging. Several years ago, the chairperson of adult studies at The Village Church assigned me the task of leading one of the classes for our Summer Series. That year we were studying people in the Bible. I could choose anyone I wanted.

"I'll do Bathsheba," I said, "in the first person." I thought I had made a mistake when I saw the look of surprise on her face as I said, "in the first person." But why not? I thought. And so I set to work.

Once I got started, I never regretted my decision, that is until the day of my presentation. For there in the class sat three of our learned pastors! Too late to turn back, I opened the session with heartfelt and earnest prayer. Then I introduced myself: "You may have heard about me before . . . I'm Bathsheba, one of King David's wives—his favorite, some say . . ."

The Lord truly blessed my efforts. I became Bathsheba for that hour, and everyone in the class had a deeper understanding and

appreciation of her because of it. "She came alive!" was the most frequent comment.

Encouraged by Bathsheba's success, I researched another woman,
and subsequently presented the woman at the well. Then I did
Martha and Naomi and Sarah and Rebekah, and the list kept growing. I began to give my presentations at other churches, resulting in
the frequent question: "Have you had your work published?"

I enjoy "becoming" the woman at the well, or Priscilla, or Leah.
Viewers tell me that the characters come alive for them. They also say
they are transported to the times and places in which the women
lived.

I have a threefold reason for the stories in *Meet Bathsheba*. First of
all, that they honor God and bless you. Second, that you come to
know these women better and develop a hunger for more of God's
Word. And finally, that you may be afforded the opportunity of pre-
senting these women yourself, in your own church. To this end, I
have included some practical "Hints for Presenters."

But, whatever your reason for reading this book, be assured that it
was written with love—for God, for the women in the Bible, and for
you. Happy reading!

Acknowledgments

The saying is true, "No man is an island," nor is any woman. This book would never have been started, let alone completed, were it not for people like my husband, Bud, who was my number one proofreader and cheerleader. I must also acknowledge the encouragement I received from Karen Schlueter, who, although she was not my proofreader, was in the stands cheering me on. Nor could I overlook the tremendous support from all of my children: Jan, Kurt, Steve, and especially, Bill, who critiqued my work so lovingly. Friends, too numerous to mention, were here to support me in so many ways. But, most of all, I acknowledge our Lord and Savior, whose love and guidance were the cornerstone of this work. To all of you, I say, "Thank you."

Hints for Presenters

I have been privileged to present "Women of the Bible" in a number of different locations, anywhere from sanctuaries to country clubs. Each setting presents its own unique challenges. Here are some things I have learned from my experiences.

Know the material. Become so familiar with the story that you empathize with the woman. Do not merely read the script, but have eye contact with your audience. Draw them into the story. You cannot do that if you are just reading to them.

Choose the setting. Sometimes the most difficult setting is the most informal. I did one presentation at a large dining room table. Women kept arriving until every place around the table was occupied and latecomers sat behind them. If you are faced with such a situation, suggest another setting, where women will not be distracted by the backs of others' heads.

Decide whether to have or not to have a podium. You will need a place for your script. The back of a chair will not do. (A glass of water close at hand is a "security blanket," too.)

Use a microphone. If the group is large, spread out, or elderly, you will need a microphone. There are times in the script when you must lower your voice for effect.

Rely on prayer. Have prayer partners who will pray during the presentation.

Create the "cast." Each of these profiles has been written as a monologue, but you may want to include other "voices" offstage for dramatic effect.

Minimize costumes and props. I have always kept costumes and props very simple: a water jar for the woman at the well, a blue wrap for Mary, a small clay dish for Martha. A piece of leather would illustrate Priscilla's profession, and a staff could represent the travels of Sarah, Rebekah, Leah, or even Naomi. Simplicity has been my hallmark, my desire being to focus on the woman and her story.

Add special touches. Here's where your individuality can shine! Do you sing? Try ending a profile with a simple chorus that ties in with the story or that extends an invitation to accept or deepen one's relationship with Christ. This can be a very effective conclusion.

Be prepared. People always want to know more! Be prepared to answer questions, but don't be afraid to say, "That's a good question. Let me look into it." But be sure to find the answer, if there indeed is one. Remember, God doesn't tell us everything!

Modify the script if it is too long. Most of the profiles take forty to sixty minutes to present. The most difficult thing for a writer is to cut anything from her work. But, sometimes it is necessary. The following suggestions might help if the material is too long for the time period allotted.

SARAH, MOTHER OF NATIONS

Sarah's story is about fifty minutes long. If there is not enough time for the complete story, you could do two twenty-five minute segments. End the first session with Abraham and Sarah's expulsion from Egypt. The second twenty-five minute presentation can then begin with the passage that follows, starting with the words, "A wall of silence existed between Abram and me for quite a while after that."

If, however, you do not have two time slots and must still do your presentation in fewer than fifty minutes, you might cut the descriptive passages about their travels.

REBEKAH, ISAAC'S LOVE AND COMFORT

Rebekah tells her story in about one hour. As with Sarah's presentation, if you have two time periods, you could do two thirty-minute presentations. End session number one with the first meeting of Isaac and Rebekah. The paragraph begins: "What a tribute Isaac paid to me, his beloved Rebekah." The second thirty-minute presentation can begin with the passage that follows, where Rebekah meets Abraham for the first time.

If you do not have two time slots, omit the section about Abimelech, king of Gerar.

RACHEL AND LEAH, SISTERS AND WIVES

Rebekah and Leah is the longest presentation. You can reduce the time to about fifty minutes if you eliminate the childbearing section. If you can present the material in two parts, a good cutoff place is the passage right before the childbearing section. The second part of the presentation should begin with the explanation of Jacob's years of servitude to Laban. The paragraph begins with the words: "The years of Jacob's servitude." In that way, you can do the presentation in two twenty-five minute periods.

If you need to do the whole presentation at one time, eliminate the first section immediately following Leah's discovery that she had weak eyes. Take up the story again where Jacob arrives at the home of Rachel and Leah. As suggested above, eliminate the childbearing section. To further shorten your presentation, eliminate the section of Dinah's rape. The paragraph begins: "We had begun to feel that Shechem was our home." Resume the story where it says: "But as always since Jacob became Israel, he heeded the word of the Lord."

BATHSHEBA SPEAKS—RECOLLECTIONS OF SIN FORGIVEN

The story of Bathsheba takes about forty-five minutes to tell. If you have a shorter time period for your presentation, cut the section that describes the Hittite people, beginning with the fourth paragraph. Take up the story again where Bathsheba explains that Uriah had every right to be proud. You may also want to cut the description of Bathsheba and Uriah's wedding. It adds color, but if you have time constraints, its elimination will not hurt the story.

NAOMI—THE ROAD TO REDEMPTION

You can present Naomi's story in about forty-five minutes. If you have two time slots, you can conclude the first part at the point at which Naomi and Ruth arrive in Bethlehem. Resume the story with the following paragraph.

If you need to do the whole story in one session, eliminate the first four paragraphs plus the section describing the famine. Resume the story where Elimelech says, "We can make it. I hear that the famine has not hit Moab."

COME! MEET MARY, MOTHER OF OUR LORD

The presentation of Mary takes almost an hour. If you do not have that long and can do it in two sessions, a good cutoff place is where Jesus comes home to Nazareth as a young boy. This was the hardest story for me to cut. However, I know that it is not always practical to include everything, so if you must cut something, eliminate the section of Mary's visit to Elizabeth. Another section whose absence won't hurt the overall story is the one describing the family life in Nazareth. I highly recommend, however, that this story be told in its entirety if at all possible.

THE WOMAN AT THE WELL—ENCOUNTER AT SAMARIA

The woman at the well story is the briefest monologue. It can be presented in approximately thirty minutes. Because of its brevity, cuts are not recommended.

MARTHA—TOUCHED BY THE SAVIOR

Martha's story can be told in about fifty minutes or in two periods of about twenty-five minutes each. Section one ends at Lazarus's tomb. Section two begins there.

If you need to do the story all at one time, but do not have fifty minutes, you can introduce yourself as Martha, Mary's sister, then eliminate the first four paragraphs. Another section you may want to cut begins with the words: "I can still remember our first meeting." Resume the story of Jesus' arrival with the words: "I opened the gate, Mary at my side, Lazarus coming up behind."

PRISCILLA—TEACHER, PREACHER, AND TENTMAKER

Priscilla is another fifty-minute story. If you can do it in two sessions, end the first one with Paul's first preaching where he concludes with the words: "Brothers and sisters, the long-awaited Messiah has come." Session two begins with the next paragraph, which begins: "Have you ever had such a thrill of excitement . . .?"

If you need to cut the story, introduce yourself as Priscilla and your husband as Aquila. Begin the story with their expulsion from Rome, saying, "Because we Jews were identified with, of all things, that mystery cult, Christianity, our life in Rome was in jeopardy." Pick up the text with the sentence that says, "I was marketing at the agora when the Roman soldier had come into our shop."

Sarah,

Mother of Nations

My name is Sarah. I am almost one hundred twenty-seven years old, and I am beginning to feel my age. I don't spend much time looking ahead, but looking back is no problem at all. Reminiscing comes naturally with old age. Abraham and I have been through a great deal in our many years together, not simply as husband and wife, but also as half-brother and sister. You see, Terah was *my* father as well as Abraham's. We *did* have different mothers, however. Don't scoff. It was the custom.

We were city folks. Our native city, Ur, was the capitol of Sumer, in Southern Mesopotamia. Ur was an important metropolis, built alongside the Euphrates River. It was halfway between the head of the Persian Gulf and the city you now call Baghdad. Abraham and I lived there while it was at the height of its glory. Our city was the place to be. Ur was the prosperous center of religion and industry.

One of the most impressive structures in all of Ur was the ziggurat. That massive structure towered seventy feet above the plain! It dwarfed everything else in the city, and boasted a system of terraced platforms, built in successive stages with outside staircases. The inside was composed of plain mud bricks. Ah, but the outside! The entire structure was finished with fired bricks that were beautifully glazed and brilliantly colored!

At the very pinnacle of this breathtaking ziggurat was the temple. It was a shrine of Nannar, the moon god, one of the most revered of all Sumerian gods. The ziggurat symbolized a mountain. The worshipers believed that the temple bridged the gap that separates humanity from the gods.

We loved fine things, and we had them. Ours was a family who enjoyed comfort and wealth. Our home was graced with exquisite china and fine crystal works of art. We were an advanced, thoughtful, cultured people. We recorded *everything* on our cuneiform tablets. It was not uncommon to hear legal decisions being declared from the door of the "Great House of Tablets." Being in such close proximity to the Persian Gulf made Ur a center for commerce and trade. I saw goods coming from everywhere, from as far away as Egypt, Ethiopia, and even India.

Religion was prominent among our people. The important gods of our land were those over heaven, the air, and the earth. Their names were Anu, Enlil, and Enki. Father Terah was devoted to the moon god, Nannar, sometimes called by the name, Sin. Legend says that Father Terah made idols to represent his favorite gods, but I won't dwell on that.

Life was placid in Ur. That is until Haran, Terah's oldest son died. Terah had two remaining sons: Abraham and his older brother, Nahor. "It is time for my sons to have wives," Terah said. He went on to announce that Nahor was to marry Milcah. I became Abraham's bride. My, that was a long time ago. At that time, Abraham was called Abram, and I was Sarai.

Nahor and Milcah were quite content to settle in Ur, but Terah was restless. Perhaps his nomadic ancestry was beckoning him to move on. "We will go to the land of Canaan," he declared. "We" meant Abram, our nephew Lot, and me.

I knew our father well. There was to be no question about his authority. "Obedience to one's father," Abram mused, "is nothing to be trifled with. Father Terah says 'Go.' We will go." We made preparations to leave our beloved Ur.[1]

The trip wasn't so bad, once I got used to living in a tent rather than in the ten-room house we left behind. We were a large company of people. Besides Terah, Lot, Abram, and me, there were all of our servants, plus all of our livestock and camels.

We headed up the Euphrates River, stopping briefly at Mari, that cosmopolitan city with its ziggurat, temples, and the most enormous palace I had ever seen. The edifice was so large that it easily boasted three hundred rooms. They were filled with beautiful art and wall paintings. And the kitchen was one that any woman of that day would love! But the most important wing of the palace housed the library. It contained more than twenty thousand cuneiform tablets. Everything from business contracts to lists of people, materials, accounts, and correspondence was recorded. There were even tablets with detailed descriptions of our divergent and infinite customs.

We were the typical tourists. I particularly enjoyed all the sights and sounds of this great city. The highlight was our attendance at a banquet honoring a city official.

"Isn't the music wonderful?" I asked Abram. Not waiting for a reply, I added, "Oh, look, Abram, see the honored guest and his entourage! How elegantly they are dressed!"

Abram condescended to my girlish excitement. "And see," he said, "the tables too are elegantly 'dressed' with all the flavors of Mari." We laughed discreetly. The party had begun in our hearts already.

I loved Mari and would have liked to stay longer. It reminded me of our home in Ur. The urban life was still in me, but the pressures of our growing "family" got us on the road again.

The final leg of our trip to Haran was rather uneventful, or perhaps the many years since then have dimmed my memory of our travels to that bustling city on the Belikh River. In any event, when we arrived at Haran we pitched our tents outside the city. We needed the good pasture land for our many animals.

"How long will we stay at Haran?" I asked Abram.

"Perhaps longer than we did in Mari," he said.

"Why is that?"

"Because Father Terah has heard that a temple to the moon god is being built here. His passion for Nannar has not diminished."

There was little doubt that moon worship and Terah went together. I could see Abram's discomfort grow with every passing year as we noticed Father's devotion to Nannar become more firmly entrenched.

There was another reality that had become a deep and growing source of concern—my barrenness. How I longed to have a child! How I desired to bear a son for my Abram. It is a disgrace for a woman not to bear a child, particularly a son. Even though our servants were enlarging our family, I could not conceive.[2]

We settled in Haran, wondering if we would ever cross the Jordan into Canaan. Still it was a cosmopolitan city, the junction of the caravan trade between Nineveh and Carchemish.

We were still in Haran twenty-five years after our arrival when Terah celebrated his two-hundred-and-fifth birthday. It was his last. Terah died. We buried the father of our clan beneath the aspen tree some distance from the town itself. How Terah had loved the quivering leaves on that stately tree. It was a fitting resting place for him.[3]

"And now, Abram, you are the head of our family," Lot reminded him.

Abram became hushed and introspective, bearing the full weight of that awesome responsibility. He spent long periods of time in quiet reflection. One day, after his meditation, he approached me. "Sarai," he said, barely above a whisper, his face aglow with some new insight gained from his contemplation. "The Lord has spoken to me," he said.

"Nannar?" I asked.

"No," he said. "Not Nannar. The *Lord*."

His face glowed as he related the words spoken by a God who was unknown to me: "'Get out of your country,' the Lord told me," Abram began. "'Leave Haran. Go from your kindred, and from your father's house. Go to a land that I will show you. I will make you a great nation; I will bless you; I will make your name great; and you shall be a blessing. I will bless those who bless you, and I will curse anyone who curses you; and in you all the families of the earth shall be blessed.'"

I could feel the sense of urgency in the Lord's commission to my husband: *"Go!"* the Lord had said. *Go? Go where? I like it here!* Rebellion rose up in my spirit.

"Did you hear the Lord's promises?" Abram asked. He didn't wait for my response. In his excitement, he recited them for me again. "The Lord said he would make me a great nation and bless me. He will make my name great and make me a blessing. And think of the protection he affords, even to those who bless me! He said he will bless them but will curse those who would curse me. And, how amazing, the Lord promises to bless all the families of the earth—through *me*. And all of this in return for our departure from Haran to go to the land of Canaan."[4]

"Abram," I finally said. "You are seventy-five years old! And me, I'm sixty-five! Are you sure the Lord told you to leave? Haran has been our home for twenty-five years."

"The Lord said, 'Go,'" Abram said with finality. "And we will go."

There was no arguing with my husband in this matter. He was determined to go to Canaan as the Lord had commanded. So, we prepared for the long trip. It took all of Abram's organizational skills to arrange for our departure. Our nephew, Lot, and indeed all of our people, had to be provided for, as well as all of our livestock. And the supplies needed for the long journey ahead of us had to be obtained.

It required a great deal of preparation and execution, but at last we were ready—and off we went again—this time southward toward Canaan, four hundred miles away.[5] We traveled slowly, pitching our tents here and there, staying as long as grazing fields held out for our flocks. Sometimes we'd even plant fields of barley or wheat for a season or two, but always with the firm intention of moving on again, drawing nearer and nearer to the Promised Land.

We made our way to the heights east of the Jordan River. We saw a number of narrow passes leading up into the mountains across the valley. The most inviting was the Wadi Farah. Its greatest draw was its natural water supply. We descended to the ford of the Jabbok before crossing the Jordan. It was there that we entered Canaan. By this time we were seasoned travelers.

In the cool of the evening, Abram and I often sat outside our tent at an oasis in the deep valley. We loved looking at the brilliant stars beaming in the black of the heavens.

"Oh, Abram," I would sigh wistfully. "Would that your Lord would grant us a son. He said he will bless you. What greater blessing is there than that a man should have a son?" I felt the tears warm my cheeks as they coursed their way in tiny rivulets.

"Don't despair, Sarai!" Abram would scold. "*You* are my blessing!" And he would squeeze my hand to comfort me.

The next leg of our journey was a difficult twenty-three miles. We made our way upward for an arduous three hundred feet, stopping at the oak of Moreh at Shechem.[6]

That venerable old tree belonged to a man named Moreh,[7] who we heard was a priest of a local Canaanite cult. But the real significance of that tree was that it was there that the Lord revealed himself to Abram.

"Sarai!" Abram called in excitement. "The Lord has appeared to me. He told me that he would give this land *to our descendants.* Think of it, Sarai, to our descendants!"

I watched in amazement as Abram built an altar to the Lord, not only to worship him but to leave a memorial of the Lord's appearance to him there by the oak of Moreh.[8]

"It shall be here for all the Canaanites to see and ponder," he said.

Shortly after that we continued our journey, heading south along the watershed. As we traveled, we could see that it formed a natural north-south route through the land.

"See the rolling hills!" Abram said at the sight. "Bethel is there, to our west, and Ai is on the east. Come let us pitch our tents."

And there, on the quiet hillside, dear Abram built another altar to the Lord. "Oh, Lord," he prayed, "this is such an arduous journey. I am still not sure I was cut out for the life of a tent dweller. Sometimes I really miss the city. Sarai does too. But you have promised blessing to me, and I believe your promises. I call upon your name, Lord. Be my guide through this Promised Land, that I may become the blessing you have promised."

The area between Bethel and Ai was very remote. There were no nearby towns or cities. Our life as tent dwellers and altar builders was a distinct separation from the Canaanites who lived in the cities and worshiped their own gods. "False gods!" Abram called them.

The Lord provided food for the animals in the brush-covered and forested hills where we made camp. But before long, water became scarce. The food supply was drying up. We were suddenly faced with a critical crisis: famine, *severe* famine.

I cried softly as I gathered my personal things together. I had grown to love this land and really did not want to move on. "Abram, isn't *this* the Promised Land?" I asked.

"Yes, Sarai," he replied. "But this is only a part of it. And now, we have no choice; we must move on. I think that if we move further south, we may find good pastures again."

So, south we went, along "the way of Shur," a direct and open route through the Negeb—a well-traveled route, even then.

As we neared the land of the pharaohs, we saw as many Egyptians as Canaanites. I overheard Lot tell Abram, "I notice that these women do not have the striking beauty that the women of Ur possess."

"You're right, Nephew!" Abram replied. "And it makes the beauty of your Aunt Sarai all the more noticeable!"

I felt my heart quicken within me as I heard these words, for what woman does not love the compliment of her husband?

We had almost reached the land of Egypt. I noticed how distracted and apprehensive Abram was becoming. He was not himself.

Why, he has not spoken of the Lord for some time, I reflected. As I pondered these things I became apprehensive myself.

"Sarai," he said softly, "I have a great favor to ask of you."

"What is it, Abram?" My apprehension reached new dimensions.

He cleared his throat as a preamble. "Sarai, you are a beautiful woman."

"Why, thank you, Abram." I said as I lowered my head in a sign of humility. My apprehension turned to dread.

"But, Sarai," Abram continued. His voice sounded strained. "The Egyptians will see that you are uncommonly beautiful, too! And I'm a dead man if they realize that I am your husband. It is not unusual for a pharaoh to kill the husbands of the women he desires." He cleared his throat again. "Oh, Sarai, please, do me the service of telling them that I am your brother. That is true, is it not? After all, Terah was both your father and mine. And if you call me Brother rather than Husband, they will treat me kindly and well, rather than capture and slay me."

I was incredulous. After all these years of marriage! I could be thrust into Pharaoh's harem, and Abram could—well, I didn't know *where* Abram would be thrust. How could I refuse? If I denied Abram's request, I would surely become a widow and become part of Pharaoh's harem anyway.

"Oh, Abram," I cried. "Why, oh, why did we ever come down to Egypt?"

He could not answer. I had never seen him so distraught. He was clearly shaken by the events and deeply concerned about what would surely happen next if I refused to do as he asked.

Before I could respond, we were escorted into Pharaoh's court.

Bowing low, Abram spoke in a voice I hardly recognized. "Greetings, Pharaoh. We are from the land of Sumer, beyond the Jordan River. We have traveled all through Canaan and have come to your illustrious land because of the great famine that has spread throughout the land of Canaan." He bowed low again. "I am Abram."

As Abram straightened his frame, I lowered my eyes in an attitude of obeisance before the throne. "Greetings, Pharaoh," I said. "All that my brother, Abram, has said is true. We have traveled long and far since we buried our father, Terah, in Haran across the Jordan River."

My heart sank because I could see undeniably that the eyes of Pharaoh lusted after me. I trembled in my distress. I had responded to Abram's request.

And then, before I could gather my wits, I was ushered into Pharaoh's harem by two of his aids. The quarters were beautiful, but my heart was heavy with doubts and questions. *Would I ever see Abram again? Would his Lord intervene for us?*

Days passed, and I lived in luxury reminiscent of Ur. I was adorned in beautiful clothing and exquisite jewelry. An Egyptian girl, Hagar, was presented to me as my personal maid.

Rumors began to abound in the harem that some sort of a plague was sweeping the nation.

"There is widespread panic among the people of the land." one of the maids told me.

However, *I* had never felt better physically in my entire life than I did then.

Finally, I was ushered into the throne room. There was Abram! I wanted to shout out his name but did not dare. It was clear that the meeting had already begun.

Pharaoh's face was purple with rage. "What have you done?" he demanded of Abram. He jumped to his feet, as though ready to attack my hapless brother/husband. "Why didn't you tell me that Sarai is your wife? Why were you willing to let me marry her, saying she was your sister?"

Abram, who was usually so articulate, could say nothing.

"You have brought evil upon us, Abram! Our whole nation is suffering a plague, a mysterious pestilence. And all the while your people flourish!" Pharaoh shouted. Then, arm extended, finger pointed menacingly, he roared, "Take her—and all the gifts I gave for her. Go! Be gone!"

Pharaoh was a man of action. Without further comment he had his royal guards escort us to the Canaan border. He really meant for us to be gone! All of Egypt was glad to be rid of us.

A wall of silence existed between Abram and me for quite a while after that. I was hurt and confused. Abram was—well, I don't know what Abram was at that point. I kept my thoughts to myself, and so did he. *While we were in Egypt, there was no tent, and there was no altar.* I mused. *With no tent and no altar to set him apart with the Lord, Abram allowed the life and culture to dominate him. He was separated* from *God, not* for *him. And there was no communion between them.*

I finally broke the silence. Someone had to. "We were not abandoned," I told Abram.

"I know," he said. "The Lord provided the plague, so that we could escape and, in spite of everything, we can still become his special people."

I, for one, was really pleased and relieved to be back in the hills of Bethel and Ai. Tent life did not seem so bad to me anymore. We were family again. But still, I had the ache of being childless. "Oh, to have a son!" I cried.

Even in my barrenness, our family had grown. Lot was wealthy in sheep and oxen and cattle, too. His herdsmen seemed always to be at odds with Abram's men. It was getting tiresome to hear their constant wrangling and quarreling.

"Sarai," Abram said after a particularly difficult morning, "something has to be done. I am going to have a talk with Lot. We've got to come to some resolution to this problem or it will damage the relationship between Lot and us."

"Yes, I know, Abram," I agreed. "But what can be done?"

"We're going to have to separate from each other. We are just getting too big to remain together. We'll have to settle in different areas."

Just then we saw Lot approaching.

"Well," Abram said with a sigh, "now is the time. It cannot wait any longer." He got up from his cushion and motioned to Lot to join us. Lot bowed low before his revered uncle.

"Lot," Abram began, putting an arm around his nephew's shoulder, "this fighting between our men has to stop. Here we are, facing danger from the tribes of Canaanites and Perizzites, and still our men cannot get along as kindred should."

Nodding his head, Lot said, "I couldn't agree more. But what can we do? We have tried everything."

"Well," Abram said, "we cannot afford to let a rift develop between our clans. Close relatives such as we are must be united and harmonious."

"I'll have another talk with them," Lot offered.

"We've tried that, Lot. It did not work, but I have a plan. I think it is the solution. You take your choice of any section of the land you want, and we will separate." Abram pointed out to the east. "If you want that part, then I'll stay here in the western section. Or, if you want the west, then I'll go over there to the east."

I have often wondered at Abram's generous offer. I saw Lot gaze covetously at the fertile plains of the Jordan River, lush and well-watered everywhere. The whole section was like the Garden of Eden or like the beautiful countryside around Zoar in Egypt. The western section, on the other hand, was far less fertile and it was mountainous besides. Clearly, the eastern section held the most promise, except for its close proximity to the Canaanites.

Lot's choice was not a surprise. Preparations were made immediately. This was one time his herdsmen did not grumble. Why? Because our nephew had chosen the lush Jordan valley to the east. That is where he went, taking his large family, flocks, and servants with him.

"I will go as far as Sodom," he told us as he departed.

After Lot was gone, the Lord spoke to Abram again.

"I think the Lord approves of our separation from Lot," he told me. "It seems that every time there is a separation, he talks with me."

"What did the Lord tell you?" I asked.

"He renewed his promise. The Lord said, 'Look as far as you can see in every direction, for I am going to give it *all* to you and to your descendants. And I am going to give you so many descendants that, like dust, they cannot be counted!' The Lord told me to walk carefully in all directions to explore the new possessions he is giving us."

Shortly after that, we were on the move again. This time we moved our tents to the Oaks of Mamre, near Hebron. I was overjoyed to see Abram build an altar to the Lord.

I joined him beside the memorial and said, "How thrilled I am to see you once again building an altar! I feel a rush of hope, such as I have not felt for a long, long time."

Still that old apprehension was there. *What about Abram's descendants?* my heart cried. With each passing day, it seemed less likely that I would be the mother of those descendants.

While we were still at Mamre we got news that war had broken out. "Lot and all of our relatives and their belongings have been carried off!" Abram announced. "I must go to his aid!" Abram got an army together, and the three hundred nineteen men left, bound for Laish, where they planned to attack the attackers in the hope of rescuing Lot and all who had been taken with him.

I spent several anxious days and weeks, thinking of little else but Abram and his men. Those of us who had stayed behind tended our flocks and kept our routine. But nothing is normal when your husband is not there with you. Then, late one afternoon, I noticed someone approaching from the north. I watched anxiously as the curls of dust rose in circling patches. I stood transfixed until Abram and his fighting men finally rode into our camp. Abram was exhausted, but exhilarated by the events.

"You know, Sarai," he told me later, "the Lord is so good to me. But he is also so mysterious."

"How is that, Abram?" I asked.

"Well," he began, "on the way back from Laish, when we neared the Brook Kidron at the Valley of Shaveh, I met an extraordinary man."

"Who was he?"

"His name is Melchizedek. He is a king, but he told me that he had agreed to be a priest of the Lord, of El Elyon, God Most High, the possessor of heaven and earth. This Melchizedek gave me bread and wine. It was a special experience."

"What made it so special?" I asked.

Abram paused, smiling. "He blessed me with an extraordinary blessing: 'The blessing of the supreme God, Creator of heaven and earth, be upon you, Abram; and blessed be God, who has delivered your enemies to you.' Sarai, Melchizedek was a special messenger from God! God sent him to bless me. I gave him one-tenth of the spoils of victory. The Lord compelled me to do so.

"And then," he continued, "the Lord himself spoke to me in a vision." Abram looked skyward as he repeated the Lord's words: "'Don't be fearful, Abram, for I will always defend you. And I will give you great blessings.'

"And Sarai, I said to the Lord, 'O Lord, Yahweh, what good are all your blessings when I have no son? For without a son, who will inherit all my wealth? A servant?' Then Yahweh told me, 'No! No one else will be your heir, for you *will* have a son to inherit everything you own.'

"Oh, Sarai, what a glorious experience. God took me outside beneath the nighttime sky and said, 'Abram, look up into the heavens and count the stars if you can. Your descendants will be like that—too many to count!'

"And my dear, I believe God! And there was so much more that God told me in that vision. I shudder when I think of how he told me about our descendants and how they would be oppressed. They will be slaves in a foreign land for four hundred years. But, Sarai, God made a covenant with me. That covenant gives all this land to our descendants, the land all the way from Egypt to the great Euphrates River." He made a sweeping motion indicating the vast space of land God promised our descendants.

"Oh, Abram," I cried, "I know that the Lord is with you, but I am so sad. Why has he closed my womb?" Suddenly I was struck with the thought of a solution. I rose to my feet. "My handmaid, Hagar! Why have I not thought of this before? Since the Lord has given *me* no children, take my handmaid, Hagar—and *her* children shall be *my* children!"

I did not wait for Abram's response but set off immediately in search of the girl.

Abram did as I suggested, and the inevitable happened—Hagar became pregnant. She had been such a sweet girl, even for an Egyptian, but how she changed when she knew she would give Abram a child! She was unbearable, and she made my life unbearable. When I could stand it no longer, I went to Abram.

"This is all your fault, Abram," I accused. "Now this slave of mine is pregnant, and she despises me, even though I myself gave her the privilege of sleeping with you. Let the Lord judge between you and me!"

He threw up his hands in frustration and said, "Do whatever you want with Hagar. She is your servant. Punish her for her arrogance toward you!"

So I did as Abram suggested. I punished my handmaiden. But when I beat her for her haughty presumption toward me, she ran away. Once she was gone, I had some misgivings about my harsh treatment toward her. But I reminded myself of her rude behavior, and that soothed my aching conscience. It wasn't long, however, before Hagar returned to the camp.

"Well," I greeted her sarcastically, "I see you have returned. You know where you belong, don't you!"

"Yes," she replied, head lowered. "I have returned. But I came back because an angel found me beside the desert spring along the road to Shur. He told me to come back and to submit to your authority." She raised her head then and looked into my eyes with a defiance that startled me. "The angel told me that the Lord had heard my misery, but he said that I would have more descendants than I could count." She gloated further by telling me that the child she was carrying was a son. "A wild one—free and untamed," she said. "Like a donkey. He will be named Ishmael because God hears."

I was seventy-six years old then, and Abram was eighty-six. We were *all* miserable. I relearned an old lesson: nothing is harder to bear than broken relationships.

Thirteen years went by, in the blink of an eye it seems. Year after year flew by with nothing but silence from the Lord. I had all but forgotten the promises he had made to Abram. Sometimes it seemed as though they were only dreams. *Did the Lord really make a covenant with Abram?* I pondered in those quiet twilight hours. One evening, as was his habit, Abram strolled beyond our camp into the darkening desert. He seemed to be gone longer than usual. I had begun to feel the chill of apprehension when at last I saw him returning, almost at a trot. *How foolish*, I couldn't help thinking. *Does Abram forget his ninety-nine years?*

"God appeared to me again!" he said breathlessly as he neared. "'I am God Almighty,' the Lord said. 'Serve me faithfully and live a blameless life. I will make a covenant with you, by which I will guarantee to make you into a mighty nation.' I fell on my face in the dust," Abram said. "But the Lord continued talking. He said that I will be the father of not only one nation, but a multitude of nations. And he changed my name. It is no longer Abram,[9] but Abraham,[10] for the Lord promised I will be the father of nations. And you, my dear, are no longer Sarai, but Sarah, for you are the princess. The Lord will bless you Sarah. He said so. And he will give me a son—from *you*. Sarah, the Lord will richly bless you and make you the mother of nations. Many kings shall be among your posterity!

"Oh, Sarah," Abram exclaimed, "I threw myself down in worship before the Lord, but I have to tell you that inside I was laughing in disbelief. Me? A father? Ha, ha, ha. Me? One hundred years old? And you, Sarah, for you to have a baby at ninety? So, I said to God, 'Yes, Lord, do bless Ishmael.' But God said, '*No,* that's not what I said. *Sarah* shall bear you a son, and you are to name him Isaac[11] and I will sign my covenant with him forever and with his descendants. My contract is with Isaac, who will be born to you and Sarah next year at about this time."

Don't ever think that God does not keep his promises. He is so faithful. I find it difficult to understand because of my unfaithfulness. I remember the day that Abraham had the conversation with the Lord regarding Sodom and Gomorrah.

"God called me his friend!" Abraham beamed. "Can you imagine bargaining with God? But I did. Oh, I was most polite, and humble too. And never, not for an instant, did I consider myself on the same level with the Lord, but I did speak frankly with God. My relationship with Yahweh is very precious, not only to me, Sarah, but it seems to the Lord as well."

Abraham told me the reason for their conversation: Sodom and Gomorrah.

"I wish Lot had never moved into Sodom, that depraved city of shame and violence!" I cried.

"Well," Abraham reported, "he is not there any longer."

"Why? What happened?"

"Two angels rescued him, his wife, and his daughters before God rained down fire and burning sulfur on Sodom, and on Gomorrah as well," Abraham said, shaking his head in disbelief. "It is such a shame about Lot's wife, though," he added sadly.

"Why? What happened to her?" I asked.

"The angels warned them not to look back as they were fleeing, but she did not listen to them. Sarah, she has turned into a pillar of salt!"

"Oh, no!" I said.

"When God tells you to leave evil, you should never look back," Abraham observed.

I'm getting tired now. There were many other things that happened to Abraham and to me. How could it be any other way in one hundred twenty-seven years? I try to forget some of the unpleasant things in our life together. Like when, for the second time, Abraham denied that we were husband and wife. This time, it was when we had settled between Kadesh and Shur at a place called Gerar. The king of that region, Abimelech, sent for me late one evening. I was brought to his palace to be his bride. Imagine that! Almost ninety years old, and still so desirable! But again, the Lord intervened and the truth was disclosed. I was able to leave the confines of Abimelech's harem.

God's faithfulness knows no bounds, no limits. When Abraham and I were reunited, wonder of wonders, I became pregnant. It is still hard to believe, even when I look at my wonderful son, Isaac. Such a miracle!

But, wouldn't you know! Hagar was still a thorn in my side. I recall the day we celebrated Isaac's weaning. There was Hagar, along with her son, Ishmael, scoffing and ridiculing my dear little Isaac. She had not changed since she first became pregnant.

I remember every word I said to Abraham. I did not try to hide my feelings. "Get rid of that servant and her son!" I shouted. I could not even say their names in my anger. I told Abraham that Ishmael was not going to share the family inheritance with my son, Isaac. "I will not have it!" I cried in frustration. We sent them packing.

And I remember a fine spring day, some years ago, when Isaac was a young lad—so full of life. Oh, how I love that boy. How Abraham loves that boy! God used that love to test Abraham. I thank our Lord that I did not know about the test until afterwards.

Abraham and Isaac went to the land of Moriah to sacrifice to the Lord. When they left, I did not know that *Isaac* was to be the sacrifice!

With tear-dimmed eyes, Abraham related the events later. He told me that as he and our son walked up the mountain, Isaac became puzzled. Something was missing. He said: "Father, here is the wood, and here is the fire, but where is the lamb?"

How prophetic Abraham was when he replied, "The Lord will provide."

And our faithful Lord *did* provide! Just as Abraham was about to plunge the knife into our son's heart, a ram appeared. It was stuck in the thicket by its horns. *It* would be the sacrifice! Faithful Abraham was tested by the Lord, and he passed with true nobility!

"I came down the mountain with our son," he said. "I came down with the words of the Lord Who Provides ringing in my ears. They will forever warm my heart: 'By myself I have sworn,' says the Lord, 'Because you have done this thing, and have not withheld your son, your only son, in blessing I will bless you, and in multiplying I will multiply your descendants as the stars of the heaven and as the sand which is on the seashore; and your descendants shall possess the gate of their enemies. In your seed all the nations of the earth shall be blessed, because you have obeyed my voice.'"

Isaac was just a lad then. He is almost thirty-seven years old now. He has grown into a fine man. I know that he will marry and have children for I remember and trust God's covenant with Abraham: "I will give you millions of descendants. . . . I will continue this everlasting covenant. . . . It will continue between me and your offspring—forever."

I have learned that with God all things are possible. After all, he took a sinner named Abram and made him Abraham, the Father of Nations. Abraham learned that although it is not always easy, it is always right—obey the voice of the Lord and you will be blessed beyond your wildest dreams.

And he took a sinner named Sarai and made her Sarah, the Mother of Nations. I learned you can trust God because he is faithful and true. Thank you, Lord, for the lessons you teach. Forgive me for being such a slow learner.

NOTES

1. Genesis 11:27–31, paraphrased
2. Sons were more highly prized than daughters in that culture.
3. Genesis 11:32, paraphrased
4. Genesis 12:1–3, paraphrased
5. Genesis 12:4–5, paraphrased
6. Genesis 12:6, paraphrased
7. *Moreh* means "teacher" or "soothsayer."
8. For the rest of the biblical account, read Genesis 12:7–22:24.
9. *Abram* means "exalted father."
10. *Abraham* means "father of nations."
11. *Isaac* means "laughter."

CHAPTER 2

Rebekah,
Isaac's Love and Comfort

It has been many long years since I lived in the presence of the ziggurat in Haran in Aram-naharaim. Towering seventy feet above the city, the ziggurat dominated all of life, dwarfing everything in its shadow. Its terraced platforms were built in successive stages with outside staircases. It was made of plain mud bricks on the inside, but the bricks on the outside, for all to see, were finely fired, glazed, and beautifully colored.

The ziggurat symbolized a mountain, with the temple on top, bridging the gap that separates humanity from the gods. Worship was *the* most important part of our life in Haran. Being religious people, we had numerous gods, all of them revered and respected. But Nannar, the moon god, was the patron god of our city, so he was the most honored and worshiped of all.

"Rebekah," my father would say. "Your Great-grandfather Terah traveled to this illustrious city many years ago to be near this ziggurat and worship the moon god, Nannar."

"What of Uncle Abraham?" I would ask. "He left Haran. He was no longer under the protection of Nannar."

A sigh from the depths of his soul prefaced his answer. "My uncle left the shelter of Haran and Nannar to follow another god. Our family has not seen him since."

Uncle Abraham and my grandfather, Nahor, were brothers. My father, Bethuel, was Nahor's son. At one time, for about twenty-five years, the whole family lived in Haran where I was born.

"Why did he leave?" I asked.

"Uncle Abraham told Grandfather that he had to. He said he had to obey the voice of the Lord. 'I will go to the land that the Lord will show me,' was all he said. Beside Sarah and all their belongings, he took his nephew Lot with him. They headed for Canaan."

Life in Haran would have been rather uneventful, were it not for the temple and our worship. We felt secure as we celebrated our seasons and our feasts at the Moon Temple atop the ziggurat.

Ours was a large family. Besides my father, Bethuel, and mother Milcah, I had eight brothers. Father's concubine, Reumah, and her four sons were also part of our family. The daily routine was rigorous but there were many hands to carry out all the tasks.

One of my responsibilities was drawing water from the spring located just outside the city. Early one evening, along with other girls from our district, I approached the well.

Life, as I had known it, was about to come to an end. The changes began with a man. He was standing there, beside the treasured watering spot. He had many camels. They were kneeling in their traditional fashion. The man raised his eyes to the darkening skies. He appeared to be praying to some unseen God.

I was startled when he lowered eyes, surrendering his reverie. "Please, miss," he said quietly as his eyes met mine. "Would you be so kind as to draw some water for me? I thirst and a drink would be most welcome."

I did not recognize the stranger. He had a weather-worn but trustworthy face. Weariness etched his eyes and the corners of his mouth. *His journey must have been long and hard,* I surmised.

"I am most happy to draw water for you, sir." I said.

He brightened as I added: "And I'll get water for your camels as well. They too must thirst."

He gratefully drank the cool refreshment. Then I filled the trough with water, over and over again until the camels were satisfied.

It must *have been a long journey,* I thought to myself. He never said a word, but I could feel his eyes watching me as I completed the task.

"There," I said at last, putting my water jug on the dusty path. I drew a sleeve across my perspiring forehead. "All done."

He was smiling now, wrinkles creasing the corners of his dark eyes. He reached into his saddle bag, his fingers caressing shiny objects.

"You have been most helpful," he said, handing me a ring and two bracelets. "I want to thank you. Your kindness went beyond what one could expect."

"Oh, but sir," I cried. "I did this kindness because it was my desire to do so. I did not do it for my gain, but for your need!"

His hand still extended with the lovely gifts, he continued, "Here, gracious lady, please take my gift."

Reluctantly I extended a hand to accept the golden treasures.

"Whose daughter are you?" he asked as he placed the ring and bracelets in my hand. "Do you think there would be room in your father's home tonight for a weary traveler?"

His request was not uncommon, nor was my response.

"My father is Bethuel," I answered. "We would be honored to have you stay with us. Yes, sir, we do have room in our home for you. And besides, we have plenty of straw and food for the camels."

His smile broadened as he thanked me. He lifted his eyes skyward and raised his hands in an attitude of worship. I marveled to hear his prayer: "I thank you, Lord God, for my master Abraham."

Abraham! Could he mean Father's uncle? I pondered.

The man continued praying aloud: "Thank you, Lord. Thank you for being so kind and true to him, and for leading me straight to the family of my master's relatives."

I felt a rush of excitement at this wonderful turn of events. Family is so important to us in Haran—almost as important as the worship of Nannar. I ran home to tell my family about this man and his request for supper and lodging. When I arrived, out of breath, I found my kindred all assembled. *They are all together as though waiting for me,* I marveled.

"There is a man by the well," I said between gasps. "He needs lodging."

Even before I finished my tale, my brother Laban rushed out to get the man who was waiting with his camels at the spring. There was no missing the glint of greed in Laban's eyes when he saw the gold ring on my finger and bracelets on my arms. He fairly bolted past me and down the path leading to the well.

It wasn't long before they made their way up the path toward our home, Laban and the stranger in the lead. "It is good for you to be here," I heard my brother say. "Why stay outside the city? We have a room all ready for you. And there's plenty of room for all of your camels too!" Laban gestured in a great sweep, encompassing the entire group.

At last all were gathered about the dinner table. A hush fell over the family as the man stood up from his cushion beside my father. All eyes were upon him as he spoke softly: "You are so kind. My heart overflows. But, I cannot eat, friends. No, not one morsel shall pass my lips, not until I tell you my mission. With your kind permission, I must tell you why I am here."

Laban was always the quickest to respond. It was no exception that evening as he rose to his feet, saying, with impatience coloring his words, "All right, then, friend. Tell us your errand."

The stranger bowed low, his head almost touching the ground. He straightened and looked about at all the curious eyes focused on his resolute face. "I am Eliezer, Abraham's servant," he explained. The shock of hearing Abraham's name was evident on every face. Everyone, without exception, sucked in his breath at the astonishing announcement.

Eliezer continued: "And the Lord has overwhelmed my master with blessings, so much so that he is a great man among all the people of his land. God has given him many flocks of sheep and herds of cattle, and a fortune in silver and gold, and many slaves and camels and donkeys."

He cleared his throat, focused his attention on Father, and said, "Now when Sarah, Abraham's wife was very old, she gave birth to my master's son. My master has given him everything he owns. He made me promise not to let his son, Isaac, marry a local girl in Canaan, but to come to his own relatives here in this far-off land. I promised Abraham that I would come to his brother's family, and," he added with passion, his eyes now resting on my upturned face, "to bring back a girl from here to marry his son."

He continued to relate his conversation with Abraham. "'But, Master,' I said to Abraham, 'what if I cannot find a girl who will come?' 'She will come!' he answered me. 'For my Lord, in whose presence I have walked, will send his angel with you and make your mission successful. Yes!' Abraham told me, 'Find a girl from among my relatives, from my brother's family. You have promised. You are under oath.' My master is a fair man, and he said to me, 'But if they won't send anyone, you are freed from your oath.'"

Eliezer paused. He looked into every face in the room, each mirroring astonishment. Satisfied that we were listening intently, he continued. "This evening, when I came to the spring, I prayed, 'O Yahweh, the God of my master, Abraham, if you are planning to make my mission a success, please guide me in this way: Here I am, Lord, standing beside this spring. I will say to some girl who comes out to draw water, 'Please give me a drink of water!' And if she will reply, 'Certainly! And I will water your camels, too!' let that girl be the one you have selected to be the wife of Isaac.'

"How faithful is the Lord!" Eliezer said, "For while I was still speaking these words, you, Rebekah, were coming along. I watched you approach with your water jug upon your shoulder. You went down to the spring and drew water. I asked you for a drink, and you answered just as I had prayed you would."

His eyes met Father's. Eliezer smiled broadly as he told Father, "I asked her about her family and learned that she was your daughter. So, Bethuel, I gave her the ring and the bracelets. Then I thanked Yahweh, the God of Abraham, because he led me along just the right path to find a girl from the family of my master's brother."

Eliezer wiped a stray tear from his dark eyes and said, "So tell me, yes or no, will you show kindness and faithfulness to my master? Please tell me, so that I may know which way to turn."

The marriage proposal was the strangest I had ever heard. I sat there, transfixed. I knew that my life weighed in the balance of the decisions being made here.

Questions flooded my mind: *What would it be like, so far away from my home and everything I held dear? Would I even like Isaac? What was he like? What about his household? What would my life be, once I left the comfort and security of my father's home?*

The palms of my hands felt damp, clammy. I bowed my head and lowered my eyes as I listened to the response of my father and Laban: "This is from the Lord. It is clear that he brought you here, so what can we say?"

Laban came alongside me, and in a gesture of affection, took my hand in his as our father said to Eliezer: "There is Rebekah. Take her and go, and let her become the wife of your master's son, just as the Lord has directed."

Eliezer beamed with delight. He bowed down and worshiped the Lord. Everything was happening so fast! He opened a sack and took out jewelry and beautiful clothing.

"Here, Rebekah. These are for you!"

He had gifts for everyone. Mother was given a beautiful bracelet and jewels for her hair. My father received a golden goblet. Each of my brothers received gifts of unspeakable beauty and value.

Supper turned into a festival. The men around the table were in the highest spirit. I pondered the situation. I found myself praying to Abraham's God. *It is certain that he has more power than Nannar, the moon god.* I decided.

A strange peace overwhelmed my soul. The mighty God of Abraham and Isaac was to be my God, too. I looked forward to my new life in Canaan, anticipating exciting new vistas.

On the following morning, before the rising of the sun, Eliezer and his men prepared to leave. He was excited about the success of his mission and was eager to return to Canaan and his master, Abraham. The camels were loaded with their burdens for the journey.

Mother was not so eager for our departure, for it meant losing her daughter to the unknown world of Canaan. All she knew about the land was what she had overheard in bits and pieces from caravan travelers who traversed the land around Haran.

Yet, I was surprised at her plea to Eliezer. She clutched at his sleeve, a bold and unseemly gesture for a woman. She implored him with tears of anguish, "Please, sir, let Rebekah stay with us, just for ten days or so. And then, as you must, you may go."

But Eliezer was just as impassioned, as he pleaded with my distraught mother, "Please, Milcah, do not detain me. The Lord has blessed me with success in my journey. Send me on my way, so that I can hurry back and tell my master, Abraham."

"I will grant you this much, Eliezer," she responded. "I will confer with Bethuel and Laban." Eliezer agreed and waited with his camels as Mother came inside to speak with Father and Laban.

"Please, Bethuel," she began. "Eliezer wants to depart—*now!* Can we not have our girl for a little while longer?"

As the three of them conferred, they decided that I should be included in the final decision. Father turned to Abraham's waiting servant. He said with a note of finality, "We will call Rebekah. We will ask her what she thinks."

I had already made my decision. Having the peace of God, I answered simply, "Yes, I will go."

Mother was very quiet as she helped me prepare for the long journey. I wanted to bring along everything I valued—gifts and keepsakes and long-cherished possessions. I exclaimed over each one as held it up for Mother's inspection. But, of course, it was not possible to take everything, so more decisions, tearful decisions, had to be made. But in due time all was ready.

We stood in the courtyard—Mother, Father, Laban, and all my other brothers. It was time for the final farewells.

"Oh my little turtledove," Mother cried. "I shall miss you, but may you be the mother of many nations. May Abraham's God look with favor upon my dear Rebekah."

Father crushed me to himself and whispered his love in my ear. Even Laban showed more tenderness than I was accustomed to. One by one, each brother offered me a sad farewell. The gifts had been loaded onto the camels.

My maids stood behind me, my childhood nurse, Marah, beside me. They were ready for the trip as well. Although I was no longer a child, I was greatly comforted that Marah was going with me on this, the journey of my life.

A breeze rustled through the courtyard, causing tiny swirls of dust to rise from the ground. I looked at each of my loved ones gathered around. I noticed more than one tear-stained face. It was time for my mother to lead the blessing. Her tender words were echoed by my father and siblings: "Our Sister, may you increase to thousands upon thousands; may your offspring possess the gates of their enemies."

Tearful hugs followed. We mounted the camels and were on our way southward toward Canaan, four hundred miles away. We traveled slowly, pitching our tents here and there, resting only briefly, moving on again, drawing nearer and nearer to the Promised Land and to my husband-to-be, Isaac.

From the heights east of the Jordan River, a number of narrow passes can be seen leading up into the mountains across the valley. The most inviting is the well-watered Wadi Farah. Just like Abraham and Sarah before us, we descended to the ford of the Jabbok before crossing the Jordan and there we entered Canaan. By this time I had become a seasoned traveler.

In the cool of the evening, Marah and I often sat outside our tent at an oasis in the valley, which was nearly eight hundred feet below sea level. We loved looking at the brilliant stars beaming in the black of the heavens, imagining what our family was doing just then.

"Oh, Marah," I would sigh. "Maybe Mother has taken a moment to look at the stars too!" Tears dimmed my eyes. "Oh, how I miss my dear family."

"Mistress," Marah would say. "We are on our way to a new home. And wonder of wonders, it is your family! Abraham is your grandfather's brother! Your loneliness will be dispelled when you are once again with family—a new part of your family."

But then it would be time to be on the move again.

"No time to tarry," Eliezer would say. We headed south along the watershed that forms the north-south route through the land. The area we traversed between Bethel and Ai was very remote.

We continued southward to the Negeb. It was evening when we arrived at the grazing fields of Beer-lahai-roi. It was getting tiresome, sitting up high on my camel. I was riding alongside Eliezer. I felt like asking, "Are we there yet?" because it seemed as though we'd been traveling forever. While pondering these pitiful thoughts I noticed a man some distance away. His arms were raised to the heavens. Perhaps he was praying or meditating. Just then he became aware of our presence and of the fact that we were drawing nearer. He started coming toward us.

"Who is that, Eliezer? Do you know him?" I asked.

"Oh, yes, Rebekah," he said, a smile of delight brightening his face. "That is Isaac! That is my master's son!"

So, that is to be my husband, I thought as I dismounted wordlessly from my camel. I could feel everyone's eyes upon me. I discreetly lowered the veil over my face. Then slowly, with deliberate step, my head lowered in a subdued fashion, I approached Isaac. The distance between us narrowed slowly as we moved toward one another. And then, finally, we were face to face. I raised my eyes modestly to look into his. *What beautiful eyes!* They danced with delight. His face was ruddy and strong. *I will like my husband,* my heart rejoiced.

"Rebekah!" he said. *I like the sound of his voice, strong and sure,* I thought. "Rebekah," he repeated. Then in a hush he added, "My wife!"

"Isaac," I said, my voice sounding strange in my ear. "Isaac, my husband."

"I have waited such a long time for this day," he said. *He is right,* I reasoned. Eliezer had told me that Isaac was forty years old.

Isaac took my hand ever so gently and led me to his mother, Sarah's tent. We were husband and wife from that time onward.

"Oh, Rebekah," he would say to me in quiet moments, "my love for you is a towering mountain. My heart is overwhelmed that Yahweh has brought you to me. You bring so much joy into my life. And oh, how you have been such a comfort to me, especially as I have mourned the death of my mother."

What a tribute Isaac paid to me, his beloved Rebekah. For a husband to love his wife is a blessing beyond measure, and I had the added blessing to be his comfort in his season of sorrow. I grew to love Isaac and to love his God, Yahweh. *Thank you, Yahweh, for bringing me home!* I often prayed.

I shall never forget the memorable day I met Isaac's ancient father, my Uncle Abraham. Isaac led me into his darkened chamber.

"After Sarah died," Abraham said, "I married Katurah. She bore several children, but Isaac is my son of promise. Everything I have will be his one day. Each of my other children will receive great and worthy gifts. The Lord has blessed me with abundant riches. No one will be in want. But, Isaac, my son of promise, is and forever will be my chief heir."

Abraham could always be trusted to keep his word. The day came when he did indeed give lavish gifts to all of his children and concubines. It reminded me of the day I left my home in Haran. We, too, were laden with gifts as we left.

Abraham sent his other children and his concubines to the east. "Go," he said. "And may the Lord your God watch over you and your children."

Slowly, they made their way toward Moab. Quiet permeated the camp. All the children—their games, their laughter—were gone. To add to our grief, shortly after their departure, Abraham, at the ripe old age of one hundred seventy-five, died. It was the first time I saw Isaac cry.

"My half-brother, Ishmael is here," he announced. "He has come to help bury our father in the cave where Mother Sarah was laid to rest." After the burial, Ishmael did not remain with us but returned to the land in the northeast. We never saw him again.

I often wondered what his life was like. "What has befallen Ishmael?" I asked Isaac one day after some years had past.

"The Lord has blessed him with twelve sons," he replied. "The Lord has said that they will become the founders of twelve tribes bearing their names. But I must tell you, Rebekah," Isaac added, "they will constantly be at war with one another. Yahweh foretold that a long time ago, and you can completely trust what he says."

The life I shared with Isaac was dependent on the land in which we dwelt. We remained in Beer-lahai-roi in the Negeb, blessed with abundant pasture land and water. God poured rich blessings upon us. I grew to love Isaac more with every passing year. *He is so tender. A real man, but a man of peace,* I often paused to reflect.

Of course, life is not without problems; they are always lurking nearby. There were those around us who envied our prosperity. And even more distressing was the fact I had not conceived. With every passing year, Isaac and I became more obsessed with my barrenness.

"Oh, Yahweh," I overhead Isaac praying, "Open Rebekah's womb. I pray that she will conceive and bear a son. Must I wait as my father, Abraham, waited for the blessing of a son? Visit us with your mercy, Lord. Bless Rebekah and me with a son and heir."

Once again God proved his faithfulness and mercy.

I could barely contain my emotions. "Isaac," I said softly to him one morning, turning from my weaving loom. "I have wonderful good news for you."

The smile on my face gave my secret away. "Oh, Rebekah!" he cried in joy. "The Lord has opened your womb! You are going to have a baby!"

I left my task and danced around the courtyard with my deliriously happy spouse. "Oh yes, my dear," I confirmed. "We are going to have a baby!"

How thrilling it was, the first time I felt the life of our baby in my womb. At first it was merely a feeling, an almost imperceptible tickle. But soon it became so pronounced that it was impossible for me to sleep. The movement was constant. And worse than that, it was violent. *There is a war going on inside me! What should I do? What can I do?* As a last resort, I went to the Lord with my problem.

"Oh, Lord," I prayed. "I do not understand what is happening to me. One thing I *do* know: I can no longer stand the strain, Lord. It gets worse with every passing day! Please, Lord, please help me."

I have noticed how God answers prayer. Sometimes he responds with an instant "yes." But not always. Sometimes his answer is "no," or "wait."

This time, God told me why I was having so much discomfort.

"Rebekah," he said, "the two sons in your womb will become two rival nations. One nation will be stronger than the other, and your older son will serve the descendants of your younger son."

By all that is sacred! My heart cried, *Twins! That is my problem—twins!* As time went on, however, I began to realize that the problem was much more complicated than that. God told me that the regular order of things was not to prevail in the case of my sons. The firstborn son is *always* the primary, the most important person of the clan. But God said that in the case of my sons, the older would serve the younger. How strange. And how would God accomplish this?

I never told anyone about God's words to me, but I never forgot them. They were emblazoned in my mind. I continued to suffer through my pregnancy until the day of delivery. I was glad when it finally arrived, but it was not an easy time, not at all. It was the most difficult experience of my entire life. Those two boys continued waging war, even at the very moment of birth.

What a surprise awaited my first glimpse of my firstborn, Esau. That little one was as red as a fox and just as hairy! Actually, that's why we named him Esau.[1] Right on Esau's heels was my second-born, Jacob.[2] What a grip Jacob had on his brother Esau's heel, even as they were being born! It was as though they had been fighting over who would be first. From the moment of birth, they were as different as night and day.

Isaac's heart overflowed with love for Esau. When Esau was still a very young lad, Isaac would take Esau hunting. Theirs was a mutual love. It created a powerful bond between father and son. As Esau matured, his love for the hunt only grew stronger. If Isaac was unable to accompany him, he went without his father. Esau's companions were all hunters. They would stay out in the fields for long periods of time, oblivious to wind or rain. Esau's greatest joy was the hunt. And Isaac's greatest joy was Esau.

But I remembered what God had told me. It was not Esau who should get the blessing and the inheritance—it was Jacob. *But how was God going to accomplish this?* It was a question I often pondered.

While rugged Esau was out with his hunting friends, my quiet Jacob was at home, content with life in the camp. Esau was rowdy; Jacob was gentle. Esau was careless; Jacob was cautious. Esau was impulsive; Jacob was thoughtful.

My Jacob! On top of everything, he was the consummate cook. He could take the plainest of plants and herbs and turn them into a delicacy beyond belief. Add some lamb, and he would prepare a feast fit for a king. I shall never forget the day he prepared his wonderful savory red stew. The rich, pungent aroma wafted throughout our camp.

Jacob had just added some of his secret spices to the stew as Esau returned from his solitary hunting trip. The older twin had left the camp early one morning and had been gone for several days. Then on that day of days, I saw him approaching from the west. He was stumbling along, a lonely figure, with nothing to show for his long days in the open field. I was standing beside my tent as he drew nearer. He was unaware of my presence. As a moth is drawn to a flame, his attention was drawn to the dinner Jacob was preparing.

"Jacob," Esau called to his brother when he was in earshot.

Jacob looked up from his stew and hailed his brother. "How are you, Esau? How was the hunt?"

"One look should tell you, Brother," Esau retorted angrily. "I don't know when I've had such a run of bad luck."

Poor Esau. He was frustrated, tired, and hungry. "I'm starved, Jacob." He looked longingly into the pot of bubbling meat and vegetables. He could see that Jacob, once again, had prepared a stew that had no equal.

"Quick, Jacob," Esau insisted, "Give me some of that stew. I'm starving to death!"

"Calm down, Esau," Jacob replied, stirring the stew, causing the aroma to rise in tempting currents. "What's it worth to you?" he asked, looking into the eager face of his brother.

Esau looked suspiciously at Jacob. "What do you mean, 'what's it worth to me?' "

Jacob rose from his pot so that he could look squarely into Esau's eyes. "Is this stew worth your birthright?"

Esau was angry and desperate by this time. I saw him clench his fists as the veins in his neck pulsated. "Listen, you!" he yelled at Jacob. "Can't you see that I am dying? What good is a birthright if you are dead?"

"All right," Jacob said calmly. "I'll give you this whole pot of stew. You give me your birthright. Swear to me, Esau, my stew for your birthright!"

I held my breath as I waited for Esau's answer. I didn't have long to wait. "Yes, Jacob, yes," he said in his hunger and frustration. "I swear to you, Jacob. The birthright of the firstborn son is yours. It is no longer mine."

It was accomplished. Esau had sold his right as the most favored firstborn son—for a meal!

I watched from a distance as Esau devoured the stew. When he had eaten his fill, he went into his tent and took a nap. *Could he be completely indifferent to the loss of his birthright?* I wondered.

Not long after that, we *all* began to feel the pangs of hunger. A widespread famine invaded the land. Nothing would take root and grow. Even bramble bushes disappeared. The situation became more severe with every passing day.

"We have no choice," Isaac announced after yet another well had run dry. "We will have to move to more fertile ground. I have heard from caravans traveling through here that it is better in Egypt. Come, let us leave and live."

We made our wearisome way northwest toward that faraway land. We were sustained by occasional wells in the desert, but none could support us for very long, so we never tarried but continued our quest for the life-supporting sustenance. We found it at last, in the region of Gerar.

"We will stay here awhile," Isaac decided. "We can reopen one of the wells that Father Abraham dug here many years ago. Then, after a time, we will continue our journey to Egypt."

The Lord had other plans. Late one evening Isaac returned from Abraham's well in a state of excitement. "Rebekah!" he called as he neared. "The Lord has spoken to me!"

I ran to meet him, eager to hear what the Lord had told him. "What, Isaac?" I said. "What did he say?"

"The strangest thing," he replied. "God said that we are not to go to Egypt! We are to stay right here in the region of Gerar. If we do, Rebekah, he will bless me just as he promised Father Abraham."

Isaac looked heavenward. "The Lord said that he will cause our descendants to become as numerous as the stars and that he will give them all these lands. Through our descendants all the nations of the earth will be blessed. And do you know why, Rebekah? Because Father Abraham listened to God and obeyed all that he commanded! And I too will obey. We will stay right here. We will not go on to Egypt as I had planned, because I know that God is faithful. He keeps his promises. "

When Isaac made up his mind he was not easily dissuaded, except perhaps by God. So we stayed in the region of Gerar, dreaming of the fulfillment of God's promise. Isaac thought that the fulfillment would be through our firstborn, Esau. I could not bring myself to tell him that I too had had a visit from the Lord and that I *knew* the covenant would be fulfilled not through Esau but through my Jacob.

The region of Gerar, where Abimelech, the king of the Philistines lived, was able to support us quite well. Isaac had our men reopen several of Father Abraham's wells.

We had not been there very long when I overheard the men of the town asking Isaac about me. I was stunned and upset when I heard Isaac tell them, "Oh, Rebekah—she is my sister."

"Why did you lie, Isaac?" I demanded as I came face to face with him.

"Because," he explained, "you are a beautiful woman, Rebekah. It is very likely that someone would kill me to get you. I did it as much for you as I did for me."

I held my peace. But in time Abimelech began to suspect that I was, in fact, Isaac's wife. He called for a meeting with Isaac. My husband anticipated that encounter with much apprehension. I shared that anxiety, awaiting Isaac's return. After what seemed an eternity, he entered our tent.

"It is all right, Rebekah," he assured me. "Everything is turning out for the good. I told Abimelech that I feared for my life because you are so beautiful. But still, he was very angry at the deception. He said that I had mistreated him and that someone might have taken you and slept with you and made his whole nation guilty of a terrible sin. Then," Isaac added in relief, "Abimelech made a proclamation that if anyone would harm you or me, that person would pay with his life."

God blessed us, not only with safety from the men of Gerar, but with our growing wealth as well. As our fortunes grew greater, so did the hatred of the Philistines toward us. They began filling up all the wells that Abraham had dug in the region so many years earlier. But, Isaac is a patient man, and with quiet determination, he reopened others.

Finally, the king called Isaac to yet another meeting.

Isaac told me that Abilmelech said, "Get out. Go somewhere, *anywhere!* Just get away from here! You have become too rich and powerful for us."

Isaac, a man of peace, relocated in the valley below Gerar. Our men dug wells, grazed our flocks and herds. We tried to live peaceably with all men; however, the envy in the hearts of the local shepherds was too much for them. Every well that our men dug was claimed by the resentful valley people. To maintain the peace, we moved again, this time to Beer-sheba. I loved Beer-sheba, which is where Isaac built an altar to the Lord.

It was not long before Isaac had another visit from Abimelech. I watched from where I was seated by the well as the king and his advisor, Ahuzzath, and Phicol, his army commander, entered our tent with my husband. I made my way slowly toward the meeting place, wanting to learn the reason for the visit. I heard the rustling of feet as the men found cushions on which to be seated. There was the usual distorted sound of voices all running together as they prepared for the meeting. Finally, there was a hush. I strained to hear. It was Isaac who spoke first.

"Why have you come?" he asked. "I cannot believe that this is a friendly visit. After all, you sent me away from your land in a most unfriendly manner."

I recognized Abimelech's deep, throaty voice as he preambled his request. "Look, Isaac," he began. "We can see that the Lord is with you." His companions grunted their assent as the king continued, "So, we have decided we should have a treaty."

"Yes," Phicol interrupted. "A treaty, a covenant between us."

Abimelech laid out the terms of the treaty. "Swear that you will not harm us," he said. "Just as we did not harm you." His voice softened as he continued. "We have always treated you well," he purred. "And we sent you away in peace. And now, look, Isaac, look how the Lord has blessed you!"

Isaac spoke in his usual gentle manner, assuring the king that he agreed there should be peace between them. "Stay, King Abimelech, you and your men. We will celebrate this covenant together. Yes, we will feast the occasion."

"I have never known such harmony and accord between our two peoples," Isaac told me as the Abimelech and the others left. While they were still within range of our vision, some of Isaac's men came running toward us.

"Master," one said breathlessly to Isaac, "Great news! We have uncovered another well. There is plenty of water here!"

Isaac was pleased with the news. "Ah," he responded, "we shall call this well 'Shebah.'"[3] It was then that Isaac gave the site its name, Beersheba.[4] "I have made an oath with Abimelech," he said. "But more important, God has spoken to me here, and repeated his promise and blessing."

Meanwhile, Esau, Isaac's pride and joy, spent less time in the field hunting game and more time in the village hunting pretty girls. Much to our chagrin, our firstborn became interested in Hittite women.

We were overwhelmed with grief when he boldly announced: "Father, Mother, I have married Judith, the daughter of the Hittite, Beeri." Isaac turned ashen gray at the news, but his love for Esau never faltered. But when Esau married Elon's daughter Basemath, our lives became filled with turmoil and grief. Those two women seemed to thrive on disruption. We were in constant torment.

On top of that Isaac's health was failing. He developed some serious problems in his old age. He was bedridden and half blind. He felt that he was near death when he called Esau to him. *Did the Lord arrange that I overhear their conversation?* I wondered.

Isaac told our son the obvious, that he was an old man. He went on to say, "I expect every day to be my last. Go out into the fields and hunt some wild game for me. Prepare the tasty food I like and bring it here so that I may eat it. After I have eaten, I will pronounce the blessing that belongs to you, my firstborn son. Esau, I must do this before I die."

Isaac closed his dimming eyes as Esau assured him that he would do as his father asked. I watched Esau leave our camp and head out for the open fields beyond the little knoll. I wasted no time finding Jacob.

"Listen carefully, my son. I overheard your father tell your brother, Esau, to go out in the fields and hunt wild game for him. He told Esau to prepare it and bring it to him to eat. Your father intends to give Esau his blessing before he dies. Jacob, *you* must bring your father the food, so that *you* will receive his blessing."

Jacob knew exactly what I meant, but he argued, "Mother, how do you think we could get away with that? Father would know that it is me. After all, my skin is smooth, not hairy like Esau's. I'll end up with a curse, not a blessing!"

"Come on, Jacob," I told him. "Let the curse be on me. Just do as I say. You'll see. It will all be fine."

So, Jacob brought me two young goats from the flocks. I had to work quickly; there was a great deal to do. I prepared the goats for Isaac, in much the same fashion as Esau would have done with wild game. While it was over the fire, I got some of Esau's clothes from his tent (not an easy matter, with Judith and Basemath about). Jacob was very quiet as he put Esau's clothing over his own.

"Here," I said to Jacob at last, "Let me help you get these goatskins over your hands and neck. I am certain your father will never know that it is you rather than Esau."

I stepped back to inspected my handiwork. "All right, Jacob, dear," I said, satisfied that all was ready. "Take this food in to your father. And remember, while you are with him, you are Esau—not Jacob."

Jacob trembled just a bit as he went in to his father. I held my breath and uttered a prayer that all would go well. *Are we doing the right thing?* I mused. *Of course we are!* I assured myself.

I listened at the entrance as Jacob greeted his father. My concern heightened when Isaac said, "The voice is Jacob's." Relief was restored when he added, "But the hand is Esau's."

Isaac ate the meal slowly. I kept vigil for Esau's return. *Hurry, Isaac,* I kept willing my son. *Finish before Esau's return!* Finally, Isaac had completed his meal and was ready to bestow the blessing:

"Ah," he began. "The smell of my son is like the smell of a field that the Lord has blessed." Then, at last, the blessing: "May God give you of heaven's dew and of earth's richness—an abundance of grain and new wine. May nations serve you and peoples bow down to you. May you be lord over your brothers, and may the sons of your mother bow down to you. May those who curse you be cursed and those who bless you be blessed."

It was done! It was accomplished! All before Esau came home!

When Esau returned he immediately prepared the game he had brought for his father. I watched as he went into his Isaac's tent. I knew that he would be overwhelmed with grief. I did not stay close by to hear the conversation, but when he bolted from the tent, there was no mistaking his anger. Everyone in camp could hear his bitter words about Jacob, the brother he now hated: "Jacob, the Deceiver! He shall die, the moment our father closes his eyes in death!"

Judith came near Esau and he complained to her, "He took my birthright and now my blessing! The only blessing left for me is that one day I will be free from my bondage to Usurper. I shall always hate Jacob. And he shall die for his deception!"

I feared for the life of my son Jacob.

"Isaac," I pleaded during one of his more alert moments. "We must send Jacob away. You do not want him to marry a Hittite girl any more than I do." Isaac did not argue the point, so I told him my plan. "Jacob must go to my brother Laban to find a wife for himself among our kindred. After all," I reminded him, "if he stays here, he most likely will marry a Hittite, and, Isaac, you agree that such a marriage would never do."

Isaac opened his eyes, which were filling with tears. "Oh, Rebekah, where is my comfort in my old age? But you are right. Jacob must not marry a local girl." Showers of tears streamed from my husband's clouded eyes. His voice was barely audible as he added, "I fear I will never see my son again. I feel I am losing him."

Losing a son is a tragic thing. I could say that I lost Esau, too, but in truth, I felt that I never really had him. We never had the bond that existed between Jacob and me. Esau's bitterness caused him to marry two more Canaanite women, just to spite his father and me.

My son Jacob had a life of twists and turns. But that's another story, one that perhaps his wife will tell you.

I would leave you with one thought: We should always wait for God to work out his plan. I know that I stepped in where I should not have. God works in mysterious ways, his wonders to perform. Our job is to not get in the way or try to accomplish his work for him. After all, he is Almighty God!

NOTES

You will find the story of Rebekah and Isaac in Genesis, chapters 24–27, and her death in Genesis 35:19.

1. *Esau* means "hairy."

2. *Jacob* means "grabber."

3. *Shebah* means "oath."

4. *Beer-sheba* means "city of oath."

CHAPTER 3

Rachel and Leah,

Sisters and Wives

My name is Leah. My sister is Rachel. Rachel possesses grace and poise; I am awkward and a bit clumsy. Rachel is articulate; I, on the other hand, do not find it easy to carry on a conversation. Rachel is self-assured; I am shy and uncomfortable around people, especially strangers. These qualities are directly linked to the fact that Rachel is beautiful; I am plain. Oh, it was not always like this, the differences in our social graces. Oh, no, not until I realized the difference in our physical attributes did I become so introverted.

I wish I had never overheard that fateful conversation. Rachel was about three years old; I was five or six. We had just completed our simple chores. My attention was drawn to the path leading to the well beyond Haran. I squinted my delicate eyes in order to see who was approaching. It was not until I heard their voices did I realize that it was our father, Laban, talking with Eli, his trusted steward. When I heard Father mention my name, my interest was piqued. I wish it had not been. I wish I had not heard any part of that discussion.

But, unfortunately, I did, and I shall never, ever forget Father's words: "The gods have cursed me, Eli," he said. "I have no sons, just two daughters, two of them.[1] And Leah, well, she is so plain, with such delicate eyes, no man will ever want to marry her. And what of poor Rachel? Her beauty will gain her no husband, for everyone knows the oldest must marry first."

I never heard Eli's response, for even at such a young and tender age, I understood the meaning of my father's words. I was overwhelmed with grief and horror. *Was I ugly?* I wondered. I wanted to run. I wanted to hide. I wanted no one to look upon my ugliness or see my weak eyes.

I did not run, but I did retreat into a self-imposed shell. From that day onward, I avoided people; they made me uncomfortable, awkward, inarticulate. If I had not been plain before hearing my father's words, I became plain then. He never knew how he had hurt me, but I never forgot.

I prayed that our gods would change me or keep me hidden. They did not answer my pleas. Even Nannar, the moon god, was silent though I faithfully worshiped in his temple.

One thing I looked forward to was our family visits to the towering ziggurat. Its brilliance was apparent, even to my weak eyes. I imagined the temple that crowned the edifice to be the mountain that it symbolized. I believed that the temple that graced the summit of the ziggurat truly bridged the gap that separated us from the gods. We had many gods, all of them revered and respected. But Nannar, the moon god, was the patron god of our city, so he was the most honored and worshiped of all.

But growing up in Haran was not all worship and work. Rachel and I spent many happy hours on the banks of the Balikh River playing our make-believe games. I especially liked make-believe, because it was at those times that I could, at least for awhile, put aside the reality of my plainness, my "ugliness," as I had come to call it.

Sometimes Rachel and I would sit beside the river and talk. It was easy to talk with Rachel when we were alone like that. Besides, she never seemed to notice my unsightliness. Even though I constantly drew comparisons between us, I doubt that Rachel ever did.

"I miss Grandmother Milcah," she said one day, while the breeze danced on the sun-kissed river that tickled at our bare toes. "She was so dear, and fun, too!"

"Oh, yes," I agreed. "Except for the times that she thought about Aunt Rebekah."

"Then she would cry," Rachel added.

"But Grandfather Bethuel was such a comfort to her," I reminded Rachel with a fond smile. "I often think of Aunt Rebekah myself, and of Uncle Isaac, too."

The time came, all too soon, when the girls our age began to marry. Soon, most of our friends had husbands. Rachel and I did not talk about it very much. I am certain that she knew the reason neither of us seemed to have any prospects of marriage. My introspection grew. And then, wonder of wonders, all that changed.[2]

Because of my impaired eyesight, I stayed home, where I helped Mother with the domestic chores. Rachel tended sheep. Each of us would have been content with our roles in life, if it were not for the fact that we were husbandless.

Late one afternoon, while I busied myself preparing the lentil soup we would have for dinner, I heard footsteps rapidly approaching. I looked up from my task. I heard Rachel's voice before I could see that it was she.

"Leah, Leah," she called to me. "Where's Father?"

"What is it Rachel?" I asked. "Is something wrong?"

"On the contrary," she replied. "Aunt Rebekah's son, Cousin Jacob, is here! He is down at the well. He moved the heavy cover from the well so I could fetch water for our flocks. Oh, Leah," she said, taking my hands in hers, "He kissed me! After I had watered the sheep, he kissed me, and he cried with joy!"

She danced around our courtyard in the exuberance of her delight. "But, Leah," she said, pausing from her revelry, "where is Father?"

Before I could answer, he appeared in our little circle of cheer.

"Oh, Father," Rachel cried. "What great news! Your sister's son, Jacob, is here. He is at the well. He has come all the way from Canaan. He has so much to tell us, Father. Come! We must have him stay with us."

I stood there, spoon in hand, stunned and thrilled with the news. Unable to speak or even to move, I remained fastened to the spot as Father and Rachel closed the distance between themselves and our Cousin Jacob. *What could it mean—he kissed Rachel?* I pondered. *And why would that make him shed tears?*

It seemed like an eternity until they returned. At last I heard them chattering as they approached the courtyard. Everyone seemed so happy, so excited. It was contagious. I felt the joy of Jacob's arrival too. It warmed my tender heart. When they came near enough for me to see their glowing faces, it became clear, even to my weak eyes, that Rachel and Jacob had eyes for each other, and no one else.

"What a wonderful surprise!" Father said.

"For me, too, Uncle Laban!" was Jacob's sincere reply.

After supper that evening we took our places on the cushions in the courtyard. I pulled mine against the wall in the shadows, so that Jacob could not see my ugliness. I made certain, however, that I would be able to hear every word that was said.

"It was quite a journey," Jacob began. "But it helped that Mother had told me all she remembered about the trip she made from here all those years ago when Grandfather Abraham's servant, Eliezer, brought her to Canaan to marry my father, Isaac. Of course that was a long time ago. It surprised me to learn how much she recalled."

"How did you fare?" Father asked. "Was your God with you on your way?"

"Oh, yes," Jacob said, warming to his tale. "On the very first night out I had the most remarkable dream. In it there was a stairway that reached from the earth all the way to heaven. The angels of God were going up and down on it. I looked up," he said, gesturing skyward. "And at the very top of the heavenly stairway stood the Lord! He said to me, 'I am the Lord, the God of your grandfather, Abraham, and the God of your father, Isaac.' God told me that the ground on which I was lying belongs to me. 'I will give it to your descendants,' he said. And he told me that my descendants would be as numerous as the dust of the earth!"

Jacob was clearly moved as he recalled that momentous dream. "He said all the families of the earth would be blessed through me, Uncle Laban. God said that they would be blessed through me and through my descendants. He promised to protect me and bring me back to Canaan. I knew that God was there. It was an awesome place." Jacob's voice took on a mystical quality as he added, "It was none other than the house of God—the gateway to heaven!

"So the next morning I got up very early. I took the stone I had used as a pillow and I set it upright as a memorial pillar. I poured oil over it. I named the place Bethel, the house of God. I made a vow," he added solemnly, "that if God would be with me and protect me on the journey and bring me back safely, then the Lord will be my God!"

Father rose from his cushion. He walked slowly toward the wall where I was seated, unaware of my presence for he was deep in thought. "I remember the day your mother, Rebekah, left for Canaan with Eliezer," he said. "He, too, spoke of the Lord, Abraham's God." Father turned to Jacob, then asked, "Is he the same God of whom you speak?"

"Oh, yes," Jacob replied, "The Lord is the God of Grandfather Abraham, Father Isaac, and now—he will be mine as well."

The recollection of his sister made Father pensive. "Rebekah was so beautiful," he said.

"Yes," was all that Jacob said, but I thought I saw him cast a fleeting glance at Rachel.

Is there a family resemblance? I wondered. *Is that why Jacob seems so attracted to Rachel?* I felt that I might never know.

We resumed our routine after that, but the rigidity disappeared from our familiar work-a-day habits. Jacob was the reason. He was part of the routine. He worked alongside Father with an ease that made it seem as though he had always been there. Everyone was happier. The atmosphere was lighter. Smiles came easier.

"It is good to have another man in our home and our fields," Father said, echoing sentiments of each of us.

My only anguish was seeing Rachel and Jacob together. It was clear that they loved each other. My heart went out to them—and to me. *Why cannot I be pretty, like Rachel?* I cried out in my distress. I would conjure up all sorts of dreams in which I would be wed to my own true love. Then Rachel, too, would be able to marry.

It was during one of those reveries that Father made his announcement: "I have wonderful news for all of you, and for me, too," he laughed. "Jacob has agreed to his 'wages.'" Father's deep laughter once again resounded. "My nephew has received no wages for all these weeks he has been here," Father said. "But an agreement has been made for Jacob's 'wages.'" Again Father chuckled at the mention of the word *wages*.

"Come, Laban," Mother finally said. "Tell us what Jacob's wages are to be."

"You tell them, Jacob," Father said, grinning from ear to ear.

Jacob seemed taken aback, but answered quietly. "The most precious wages of all. I will work for seven years, if you will give me Rachel, your younger daughter, to be my wife."

How can Father respond, I wondered, *for I am not yet wed?*

I did not have to wait long for Father's response. "Agreed!" he said heartily. "It is better that I give Rachel to you than to some other man. Stay here with us, Jacob."

The seven years were drawing to a close, but my confusion had not abated. I still had no husband and no prospect of one. Yet Father and Mother were making elaborate plans for a wedding feast. No one seemed the least bit concerned that the younger daughter was being married although the older remained unwed.

In the midst of the arrangements, I overheard Jacob tell Rachel, "I have served your father for seven years, but they have flown by because of my love for you, dear Rachel!" It was clear that Jacob had no doubts. *Perhaps he is unaware of our customs here in Haran. That must be it,* I decided, and resumed my help with the wedding plans.

Everyone was invited. It was the biggest celebration Mother and Father ever hosted! There was music and laughter. Our table overflowed with tantalizing food and drink. Everyone joined in the festivities with delight. Especially exhilarated were Rachel and Jacob. She was more beautiful than I had ever seen her. Jacob thought so, too. He could not take his eyes off her. And she had eyes for no one but Jacob.

The guests did not seem to notice Jacob's departure in the midst of all their revelry. Father had escorted him to the bridal tent. I knew that he would tell him, "Be patient, Jacob. I will bring you your bride."

Father returned to the festive celebration. He beckoned Rachel and me to follow him. The three of us moved away from the crowd.

"Rachel," he began seriously. "Jacob's wages are about to be paid. He has earned a wife."

Neither Rachel nor I could understand why Father told us that Jacob had earned a wife. He had already chosen one, Rachel.

"But, Rachel," Father continued. "Jacob's wife must be—Leah."

"What?" she demanded, shock and horror filling her eyes. I was dumbfounded. I found no words to question or protest.

"Leah is the older," he continued gravely. "You cannot marry until she is wed." Without preamble, he turned to me. "Leah, prepare yourself to be Jacob's bride. Here is the veil. Cover your face. Jacob must be convinced that you are Rachel. The marriage will be consummated. *Now!*" He took hold of my arm and, without another word, led me—speechless—to the wedding tent.

I slowly lifted the flap, tears of confusion coursing down my cheeks. I entered Jacob's tent. "Oh, Rachel, my love," he said. The tears became a torrent.

Inexorably, morning light began to dawn. My heart beat with such terror that it encompassed my whole being. I could feel its throbbing in my throat, constricted with dread. I could hear its pounding in my ears, drowning out all other sounds. Jacob began to stir. Wakefulness began to rouse him. With dread, I anticipated his reaction to Father's deception. I did not have long to wait. He rolled onto his back, yawned, and smiled. Jacob reached for my hand. He drew me to himself.

"Why the veil?" he laughed. "You are my wife now, Rachel. No need to hide!" With that, he tore the blue linen from my face.

His mirth turned to disbelief and horror. "Leah!" he screamed, leaping to his feet. "What is this trickery? Where is Rachel?"

He did not wait for an answer. He dashed from the marriage tent in search of my father. "Laban! Laban!" he shouted in his rage. "Where are you, you deceiver?"

I stood, transfixed beside the marriage tent, unable to stop the torrent of tears. *My tears will forever flow!* my anguished heart cried as I sobbed in my distress.

Father responded to Jacob's summons at last. "What is it, Jacob? What troubles you? Are you dissatisfied with your new wife?"

That only fueled Jacob's anger all the more. He spoke through clenched teeth. "What kind of trick is this?" he demanded. "I worked for you, for seven years—for *Rachel!* And I awake to find— *Leah!*" Chills of despair pulsated through me as Jacob spit out the words. His emotions escalated from disappointment to fury.

"Now, now, Jacob," Father placated. "Perhaps you are unaware of our customs."

"Customs? What do I care about your customs, Laban?"

"Well, you must," Father explained. "For you see, the younger daughter cannot marry until her older sister is wed." Father patted Jacob's back as he purred, "Leah will be a wonderful wife. And, when the bridal week is over, you can have Rachel for your wife as well. That is, of course," he added, "if you agree to work another seven years for me."

"You are a monster, Laban!" Jacob replied. "But your trickery has won you the day! I can do no other than agree to your vile terms." He turned and left Father standing in the dust of his retreating heels. Father's face wore a smile of satisfaction as he turned to face me in the aftermath of his victory.

"Well, dear Leah," he said, still smiling, "much has been accomplished this day. You have a fine husband whom you will share with your sister, Rachel. And, I have a wonderful helper for the next seven years. Maybe Jacob's God is blessing me, too!" He threw his head back in untroubled glee and laughed the laughter of triumph.

My wedding gift from Father was Zilpah, who would forever be my servant. One week later, Rachel and Jacob were married. Rachel's gift from Father was Bilhah, who would serve Rachel all the days of her life.

The consummation of my marriage resulted in a child. I was ecstatic. The joy of my pregnancy soothed the hurt I felt because my husband loved Rachel more than me. *That's all right,* I consoled myself, hoping that the child would bring comfort to my aching heart. *Please, dear gods, let the child be a boy!* I prayed to all the household gods, as well as to Nannar, but most of all to Jacob's Lord God.

Even in the throes of labor, my prayer was constant. At last, after hours of strain and pain, I saw the midwife hold up my child upon its delivery. "A son!" she exclaimed. The entire family rejoiced at the birth. "His name shall be Reuben," I whispered as Zilpah wiped my fevered brow. "Jacob's Lord has noticed my misery, and now my husband will love me."

Reuben was a great comfort to me. The love Jacob had for Rachel never wavered, but the Lord had given me a son, and it was not long before it became clear to me that I was pregnant again. When dear little Reuben was still a babe, the Lord blessed me with another son.

"Simeon," I said to my newborn, "the Lord heard my cry that I was unloved, and he has given you to me."

Rachel took Simeon in her arms. "Oh, Leah," she said. "How you have been blessed! You have two beautiful sons. I have none." There was no mistaking the pathos in her voice as she handed Simeon to Zilpah to look to his needs.

Then came Levi. "Surely now my husband will love me. I have given him three sons!" But the Lord was not through yet! Before long I realized that I was pregnant once again. I praised the Lord even as my fourth son, Judah, was born.

And what about Rachel during my time of triumph? My poor sister, even though dearly loved by our husband, bore no children at all, not even a daughter. When she could bear it no longer, she confronted Jacob. In the heat of their verbal exchange they were unaware of me. Because my eyesight is so poor, my sense of hearing is more acute. Consequently, I had no trouble hearing what was said.

"Oh, Jacob," Rachel sobbed. "I am in misery. I am not complete. My life is a shell. You say you love me more than Leah, but you have given her four sons. I have none. I am empty. I have nothing!"

I noticed a tiny edge in Jacob's voice. "Now, Rachel, do not be so upset," he said. "You know how much I love you."

"Do you?" she demanded. "Do you, really, Jacob? Then give me children—or I shall die!"

"What?" Jacob retorted. "Do I look like God to you? Speak with him if you want children. He is the only one who can help you."

"You *can* help me, Jacob," Rachel said. "Take my maid, Bilhah, to be your wife. The children *she* bears will be *mine*."

After that discussion, Rachel frequently questioned Bilhah. The question was always the same: "Are you with child?"

"She is pregnant!" Rachel finally told me at last. "Oh, Leah, Jacob will love me when Bilhah has a son, for Bilhah belongs to me, and what is hers shall be mine." She danced off with new spirit.

Bilhah actually had two sons, first Dan and later, Naphtali. I had not had children for some time, so I went to Zilpah.

"Zilpah," I said, "I have spoken with Jacob, and he has agreed to take you as his wife so that he can have more sons. The children you bear shall be mine." She could not object. She did not even consider it. Zilpah bore Jacob two sons, Gad and Asher.

Our family had greatly increased. Jacob was a happy man. And even though he did not love me in the same way that he loved Rachel, there was an affection for me as the mother of four sons, plus the two that Zilpah bore. Rachel claimed the two sons of Bilhah.

The Lord continued to bless me even further, for I gave birth to two more sons, Issachar and Zebulun. I was overjoyed at their births for God had given me good gifts to present to my husband. *Now, he will honor me, for I have given him six sons.* The last child I ever bore was a beautiful baby girl I named Dinah.

One afternoon, about a year after Dinah's birth, Rachel came to me with her news. "Leah," she said quietly, "I am so happy. I pray you will be happy for me."

I looked up from my weaving. "What is it, Rachel?" I asked.

"Oh, Sister," she said, "God has remembered my plight! He has answered my prayers."

"How, Rachel? How has God answered your prayers?" I asked, noting the look of joy in my sister's radiant face.

"Leah," she said, "at long last, I am with child."

Seven months later Joseph was born. At his birth, Rachel said, "God has removed my shame. He has given me little Joseph," she cooed. Then she added, "May the Lord give me yet another son."

The years of Jacob's servitude to Father had gone by quickly, for they were years filled with the activity that comes with raising a family. Rachel, Zilpah, Bilhah, and I were busy with the daily routine of seeing to the needs of our large clan. There was little time to dwell on the hurts that afflicted each of us.

"I have spoken with Laban," Jacob told Rachel and me one day. "I told your father that I want to go back home."

"What did he say?" we asked.

"He is very reluctant to let us go," Jacob said. "Your father is sure that the Lord has blessed him because I am here. It is no surprise that he realizes this, for you know how his wealth has grown, not only in his herds and sheep—he even has sons now!

"He asked how much he owes me. All I asked was that he let me go through the flocks and permit me to remove all the speckled or spotted ones, the undesirable ones. Laban agreed. It will not be much," Jacob added. "But the Lord promised to protect me and bring me back to Canaan, and I trust him. He will bless us. He will provide for all our needs."

He left us then, filled with resolve. He wanted to go home.

We did not talk much about it after that. Our life in Haran seemed to go on as it always had. *Did I imagine Jacob's resolve to go home?* I wondered.

"Do you think Jacob has changed his mind?" I asked Rachel one day as we were preparing the daily bread.

She looked up from her task. "Changed his mind about what?"

"About going home."

"I don't know," she answered. "He hasn't said anything about it for some time. Maybe we should ask him."

The next day I was surprised to see Jacob returning from the field at an early hour.

"Shalom," I greeted him as he neared.

"Where is Rachel?" I felt a pang of envy at his question.

"By the fire," I answered.

"I want to see both of you," he said. The seriousness in his voice startled me. Without a word I went to fetch my sister.

"Come with me, both of you," Jacob said when we were all together. "I need to talk things over with you. Let us go out to the field where I have been watching the flocks."

We made our way through the meadow that skirted the field where the flock was feeding. Jacob slowed his pace so that we could keep stride with him.

"The Lord has spoken to me," he said.

"What has he told you, Jacob?" I asked.

"He told me to return to the land of my father and grandfather. He said that he would be with me."

We reached the field then, and I could just barely make out the shape of the flocks that dotted the landscape. "Look at them all!" Rachel exclaimed.

"Yes," Jacob said. "Your father tricked me. He agreed that all the speckled animals would be mine, but before I could remove them from the herd, he had his sons hide them. He broke his wage agreement with me again and again. Even so, God has not allowed him to do any harm to me. For when Laban said the speckled animals were mine, the whole flock began to produce speckled lambs. Then, Laban changed his mind and said I could have the streaked ones instead. After that, all the lambs were born streaked."

Jacob laughed and added: "God has made me wealthy—at your father's expense. In a dream I had during the mating season, God said that only the streaked, speckled, and spotted males would mate with the females of my flock, for he had seen what Laban had done to me, by removing the ones he had agreed were mine."

Jacob reached out to Rachel and me. He took each of us by the hand and said, "God reminded me of the place where I anointed the pillar of stone and made a vow to serve him. He told me that we must leave this country and return to the land from which I came."

"That is fine with me!" Rachel said.

"Yes," I agreed. "There is nothing for us here. The riches God has given you from our father are legally ours and our children's to begin with. So, go ahead, Jacob, do whatever God has told you."

"Good!" Jacob cried. "Now is the time to go. Your father is some distance from here, shearing his sheep. We can be well on our way before he misses us!"

We made a hasty departure. I never turned back to look at the only home I had ever known. A new life was about to begin. We made our way as quickly as we could. We did quite well, too, considering the large company of people and animals we had. Our camels were laden with all that they could carry. Even our saddlebags were filled with as many possessions as they would hold. Our flight from Haran began easily enough, but on the tenth day, when we were in the mountains of Gilead, we were overtaken by Father and some of our relatives.

What will he do to Jacob? I despaired. I did not have long to wait. Father pulled his camel up alongside Jacob and shook an angry finger at my husband.

"What do you mean, sneaking off like this?" he demanded. "I wanted to give you a farewell party, with music and celebration for a send-off. But, no, you sneak off, so that I don't even have a chance to kiss my daughters and grandchildren shalom! I could destroy you, Jacob, and I would, except that your God has warned me against it.

"I know you long for your family. I know you must go. But tell me, Jacob, why have you stolen my household gods?"

Jacob was aghast. "What? I know nothing about your gods. Here, Laban, check and see if you find your gods among our things." Jacob flung his saddlebag open so that the contents were visible. "The person who has taken them will surely be punished!" he vowed.

Father and his relatives began the search. They looked high and low but were unable to unearth the wooden idols. Finally, they approached Rachel and me. She alone remained seated on her camel.

"I am sorry, Father," she said. "But I am in the way of women and cannot rise before you."

"Well, all right," he said. "But the search is not over, not yet!"

For all practical purposes, the search *was* over, for nothing was ever found. I watched Jacob became angrier by the moment. Finally, he could hold his tongue no longer. He turned to Father and roared, "What did you find, Laban? What is my crime? Set it all out right here before everyone. Come on, Laban, what are you waiting for?"

Jacob's tone became quieter as he said, "I have been with you for twenty long years. Did I ever, in all that time so much as touch anything of yours? Think, Laban, twenty years—fourteen of them earning your daughters and six earning my flocks! God has seen your cruelty and my righteousness. That is why he came to you to vindicate me!"

That was enough for Father. He told Jacob that they should agree to have peace. They created a heap of witness.[3] They made solemn vows of peace. I shall always remember Father's final words: "May the Lord watch between you and me when we are absent one from the other." Laban rose early the next morning, kissed Rachel and me and all of our children, blessed us, and headed back to Haran. We continued our long journey to the Promised Land. I never saw my father again.

Shortly after the resumption of our journey, Jacob came to us with news. "I have been visited by God's angels in this place," he said.

I noticed that the closer we came to Canaan, the more Jacob spoke of his God. But now, his heart seemed troubled. "I am sending messengers to my brother, Esau," he explained. "I told them to give humble greetings from me, his servant, Jacob, and to tell him I have been living with Uncle Laban until recently. Now I am coming home and hope that we can have friendly relations."

Jacob was very quiet until the messengers' return. The reply Esau sent seemed to distress my husband even further. "What did he say?" Rachel asked when the three of us were alone.

"Esau is on his way to meet us," he said, "with an army of four hundred men!"

I could feel the blood drain from my face as Jacob gave orders to divide our household into two camps. "If Esau attacks one," he explained, "perhaps the other will survive. Now, I need to pray." With that, he sought a lonely spot to be alone with his God. When he returned he said, "I have been praying to the Lord God, admitting my unworthiness and acknowledging all he has given me. I began with nothing but a walking stick, and now"—he shook his head in disbelief—"now, he has shown me his unfailing love and faithfulness."

He wiped the tears from his eyes as he told us of the generous gifts he sent to Esau in the hope that he would spare his life and the lives of his loved ones. *Loved ones!* I repeated the words in my mind. *That includes* me!

"Prepare to ford the Jabbok River," he commanded. So we continued the journey. But Jacob stayed behind, planning not to join us until dawn. He would be gone all night. With the first light of dawn, I saw him returning. *But wait. Could that be Jacob?*

"Rachel," I called to my sister. "Come quickly. It's Jacob. Something has happened to him." She emerged from the tent, peering in the direction I pointed out. My poor eyes strained to make out the facial features of the approaching figure.

"Oh, by all the gods!" Rachel cried. "It *is* Jacob!" She fled to be at his side. I followed as quickly as I could. Soon, we were all together.

"Oh, Jacob," she cried.

"What has happened to you?" I panted.

"How can I tell you such a mystery?" he said.

"Please, Jacob," I said. "Tell us what happened."

"I was all alone," he began. "All at once a stranger appeared. Why he started wrestling with me, I do not know. We wrestled all night! I was exhausted but would not give up. Then, he struck my hip and knocked it out of joint. 'Let me go!' he demanded. But I told him that I would not unless he blessed me. He wanted to know my name. My name! Can you believe that? When I told him, 'Jacob,' he said, 'Not any longer. Now your name is Israel, for you have struggled with God and you have prevailed.'

"I asked what his name was. He did not tell me. But," Jacob added triumphantly, "he did give me his blessing. Rachel, Leah, what a mystery: I have seen God face to face, and yet my life has been spared."

Later that same day, we saw a great mass of men approaching. We knew it must be Esau with his four hundred men. Jacob arranged the family into a column with his two concubines, Zilpah and Bilhah, in the front, along with their children. I was behind them with all of my children. Rachel and Joseph were behind me. We made quite an appearance, I am sure.

We watched the meeting of the two brothers who had not seen each other for all those many years. None of us knew what to expect. I admit I felt much anxiety. It would not abate until I saw Esau turn and, with his men, depart in the direction from which they had come. Jacob returned to us, saying only, "All is well. Let us move on to Succoth."

Jacob actually built a house in that hot, humid place. He made shelter for the animals as well. We did not stay very long but moved on to Shechem, where Jacob bought land. It was there, at Shechem, that Jacob built an altar and called it El-Elohe-Israel.[4]

We had begun to feel that Shechem was our home. It was an important city with caravans traversing its borders in a constant stream. Dinah made friends with some of the local girls. She frequently went into the city to see them. It was after such a visit that Hamor the Hivite and his son Shechem came to see us.

"To what do we owe such an honor?" Jacob asked.

"I have come in the hope that you will permit the marriage of your daughter Dinah to my son Shechem. He truly loves her and wants her for his wife," the king said. "Furthermore, we invite you to let your daughters marry our sons, and we will give you our daughters for your young men."

Hamor's son Shechem spoke just as Simeon and Levi joined us. "I will do whatever is required," he said. "But please be kind to me and let me have Dinah for my wife."

Before Jacob could respond, Simeon said, "Never. That can never happen."

"He's right," Levi agreed. "You are not circumcised. But, if you and all your men agree to be circumcised like we are, we will intermarry with you and live here and unite with you to become one people."

Before Jacob could object, the deal was struck, and Hamor and Shechem were on their way.

"What were you thinking?" I demanded when our guests had left.

"It will be all right," Levi said.

"Yes, Mother," Simeon agreed. "You will see. We have a solution."

A few days later their solution became clear. But even more clear was the fact that it was *not* all right. I learned that when my dear Dinah had visited the girls in the city, Shechem seized her and raped her. To avenge her disgrace, while the men of the city were recovering from their circumcisions, Dinah's brothers killed every one of them. As if that weren't enough, Levi and Simeon were joined by all of Jacob's sons, who looted the city bare! Jacob was furious. But, as always since Jacob became Israel, he heeded the word of the Lord. God told Jacob that it was time to move on—to Bethel.

"Destroy your idols, your foreign gods," Jacob commanded our entire group. "I will bury them beneath this oak tree! No foreign gods will ever accompany us again!" It was clear that Jacob would expect everyone to obey his command.

The journey to Bethel was accomplished without too much trouble. Our sons avoided their father and me the whole twelve miles.

"I have come to this place," he announced when we were all assembled, "for a specific purpose. This is the very spot where God first spoke to me all those many years ago when I left my home to go to Haran. I was fleeing my brother, Esau. God made a covenant with me here and I built an altar. It is time for me to build an altar once again to the God of Bethel. He answered my prayer then, and he has stayed with me ever since."

With that, Jacob began the work of building his altar to the God of Bethel. We watched in reverence as he completed the task. I kept one dim-sighted eye on Rachel. She was pregnant and had not been feeling too well. I was relieved that our mother-in-law Rebekah's nurse, Deborah, had joined us.

But before we could make preparations for our departure to Hebron, Deborah became very ill. I feared more for Rachel than I did for Deborah.

"Her presence with me has been such a solace," Rachel sobbed in her anxiety for the other woman.

"I know, dear," I comforted. "But she is old, and this is not un-expected."

All comfort was forgotten when Deborah died and was buried beneath the terebinth tree. "It is terebinth of weeping," Rachel said in her sorrow.

"I know you weep for Deborah," Jacob said. "But we must go on, for God has spoken to me again. He blessed me and reminded me that my name is no longer Jacob, but Israel. He told me his name: 'I am God Almighty,' he said. He told me to multiply and fill the earth. He will give to me and my descendants the land on which we tread."

Jacob set up a pillar in the place where God had spoken with him. It was time to move on.

Forgive me if I weep. My uneasiness about Rachel intensified with every mile. There could be little doubt that she had moved from discomfort to serious pain.

"Oh, Rachel," I said. "We must take time for you to rest."

"No, my sister," she said, "We must move on. We are not too far from Ephrah."[5] Just at that moment, she was seized with a pain which she could not hide. I hurried my camel's pace so that I could be alongside Jacob.

"Jacob, Jacob," I said. "We must stop."

"Why, is something wrong?" He, too, had noticed Rachel's increasing discomfort.

"Rachel's time has come," I said. "She will soon give birth."

It took no more than the mention of Rachel's name for Jacob to give the order that we were to come to a halt. Jacob and I hurried back to Rachel, arriving just as she was being helped off the awkward animal. The pangs of childbirth distorted my sister's lovely face. Tears of pain streaked her face as she bit her lip to prevent the scream of anguish to escape her lips. The midwife was already at her side and together we helped her to the bed of blankets that had been provided for her.

Hour after hour, the horror of pain gripped Rachel. She was drenched in the perspiration of her labor, with seemingly no results. I have never seen Jacob in such a state of consternation.

"How long?" he demanded. "How long must this go on?"

When he wasn't fretting or scolding, he was praying, and at last, at long last, his prayer was answered.

"Do not fear," I heard the midwife say. "Rachel, you have another son!"

The midwife's words did not prevent Jacob's fear. Her words did not abate my fear. We were fearful for dear Rachel. Her pallor was that of death. In a voice that was hardly audible, she whispered, "His name is Ben-oni, son of my sorrow." Those were her last words. She died. Jacob wept. I wept.

"I will call him Benjamin, son of my right hand," Jacob said. He wiped his tears from his eyes, but not from his heart.

He set up a stone monument over Rachel's grave, and it can be seen to this very day.[6]

We went on from there until we finally reached Hebron, Jacob's childhood home. It seemed strange, meeting Jacob's ancient father. He was even more blind than I. But I was glad I could come to know him before his death at the age of one hundred eighty. I knew Jacob's sorrow that Isaac had not had the opportunity to meet Rachel.

Most of our children were grown by then and often caused us great concern. It should come as no surprise that Rachel's oldest son, Joseph, was Jacob's favorite. He seemed to favor him even more after her death. So the appearance of Joseph's coat of many colors, all stained with blood, was Jacob's sadness, as it was mine. I thank the Lord God that Jacob welcomed my comfort, for that became my comfort, too.

Jacob had a life of twists and turns. He was once a deceiver, and then he himself became bitterly deceived. Jacob wrestled with God and his name was changed from Jacob (Deceiver) to Israel (Prince of God). He has struggled with God and with men, and he prevailed. Throughout his life, Jacob has been taught by God to trust in the Lord God. As a result, his faith grew.

Lovely Rachel was most prized by Jacob. After all, he worked fourteen years to have her as his wife. She was beautiful and bright. Perhaps she reminded Jacob of his mother, Rebekah, whom he had loved dearly.

I began my life in a shell of insignificance. My eyesight was so poor that I squinted to try to make out the shapes and forms of all that was around me. I thought that I was ugly. Perhaps I was. There was no doubt whom Jacob favored. But, as my own faith in the Lord God grew, I saw the intrinsic beauty of every life, even my own. As the Lord blessed me with children, my value grew in Jacob's eyes, as well as in my delicate ones. Jacob had seen God face to face, and his life was preserved. In my heart I, too, had seen God face to face, and my life was preserved.

NOTES

1. Boys were more highly prized than girls in that culture, although women seem to have been treated with some respect, and their opinions valued.

2. You will find the story of Rachel, Leah, and Jacob in Genesis 28:10–35:29.

3. Heap of witness: a stone set up as a pillar and heaped with other stones as a memorial to their covenant (agreement).

4. *El-Elohe-Israel means* "God, the God of Israel."

5. Ephrath is Bethlehem.

6. Rachel's tomb is about a mile north of Bethlehem and about four miles south of Jerusalem; it is still regarded with great respect.

JACOB'S SONS (GENESIS 49:1—27)

1. Reuben—dignified, but unstable as water

2. Simeon—cruel and angry

3. Levi—cruel and angry

4. Judah—a lion's cub, would rule

5. Zebulun—would dwell on the coast and be a seafarer

6. Issachar—strong as a donkey, would serve others

7. Dan—judge

8. Gad—would be overcome, but would win in the end

9. Asher—would be successful tiller of the soil

10. Naphtali—a deer, let loose (a venturesome spirit)

11. Joseph—a fruitful bough, blessed by the Almighty

12. Benjamin—would be as aggressive as a wolf

CHAPTER 4

Bathsheba Speaks—
Recollections
of Sin Forgiven

You may have heard about me before, but let me introduce myself. I'm Bathsheba, one of King David's[1] wives—his favorite, some say. I know that our beginning may not have been auspicious, but still there were times I thought we were given bad press. The *Jerusalem Journal* can sometimes go too far in its editorial license. Now, I would like you to get the facts from my perspective.

Where to begin? I suppose you want to know a little about my first husband, Uriah, don't you? He was a wonderful man, a man of valor, as a matter of fact. So honorable was Uriah that he was one of David's Valiant Men.

Uriah was a Hittite. It is no wonder he was a man of valor—the Hittites were an ancient people who once ruled an empire of great size and power.

Uriah told me that when Rameses II was the Egyptian pharaoh, the Hittites' power posed a very serious threat over that nation. They finally signed the "treaty of eternal friendship." (I can't remember how long it lasted, but certainly not for eternity.) In any event, that pact is engraved on the walls of Egyptian palaces and written on tablets of stone in the Hittite capital.

"The Hittite culture is quite advanced," my husband reminded me. "In fact," he said, "it has been for centuries. For example, our literature includes everything from great epics to extensive dictionaries. Translations of temple lists and even medical texts are available. And our art! Masterful! Magnificent! It can be seen in every conceivable form from the most mammoth sculptured rocks to the daintiest silver ring seals."

Uriah had every right to be proud of his heritage. I recall his words about the Hittite complex legal code. "I don't believe that anything was overlooked," he said. "There are laws relating to everything from assault to adultery."

Adultery. Well—that's another story.

Uriah and I married when we were very young. Our parents arranged the marriage. That's the way it was done in that time and place, you know. You married; *then* you learned to love your husband. A very good arrangement, especially the part about loving each other.

What a wedding we had! Everyone in town was invited. Uriah looked like a king in his fine robes. He wore a garland of fresh flowers on his head. His clothes were scented with frankincense and myrrh. He wore a silk scarlet sash. And his sandals! You should have seen them—beautifully figured and carefully laced. Uriah looked as though *he* could have been King David! And everyone bowed to him, paid homage to him.

I wasn't dressed like a peasant, either. My sisters and cousins helped me prepare my complexion so that it was all glossy and shining with a luster like marble. It made me think of one of King David's psalms: "that our daughters may be as corner stones, polished after the similitude of a palace."[2]

My long, thick hair was braided with gold and pearls. In fact, I was covered with all the precious stones and jewels that my family had inherited from all the previous generations. I'll never forget that day—*that week!*

At last, all was ready. I could hardly wait for Uriah to come. And then, there he was! He'd come to my father's home to get me and take me to *his*. My parents and sister, brothers, *all* my family blessed me with the words once spoken to our matriarch Rebekah: "Thou art our sister, be thou the mother of thousands of millions, and let thy seed possess the gate of those which hate them."[3]

I left my father's home with Uriah. We were followed by a grand procession all the way to his home, my *new* home. Some of my cousins ran ahead and scattered ears of parched grain to the children who lined the path. All along the way there were demonstrations of joy. The men played their musical instruments. Others were dancing. It was a festive occasion.

But, marriage moves beyond the celebration. All too soon, the sounds of the wedding fade, the guests go home, and your new life begins.

Uriah, as I said, was one of King David's Valiant Men—that group of fighting men who were the very core of the king's army—David's most trusted, valiant warriors. And my Uriah was one of them.

We lived in Hebron until we set up our home in Jerusalem. I love Jerusalem. What an exciting city!

And what a genius King David was. When he was only thirty-seven years old he was declared ruler of all of Israel. The nation was no longer divided. At the time he was crowned ruler of the united kingdom, his capital was in Hebron.

"Why does the king want to move the capital to Jerusalem?" I asked Uriah when I heard of the planned move.

"Hebron is too far south and too closely identified with Judah to remain capital of the *united* kingdom," he explained. "I tell you, David is a genius! Jerusalem is the perfect site for our capital. It is only about twenty miles north of Hebron. It offers easy access from several directions. There is no doubt, it had a lot to recommend it as the capital of a united Israel.

"You remember," he added, "that the city is located on a rocky point, shaped like a triangle. Besides that, it has deep valleys on two sides. Invasion by enemy troops will be very difficult. Jerusalem's water supply is secure. It has a wonderful, dependable spring. And to add further advantage, there is very little water in the surrounding limestone mountains to support an attacking army."

As Uriah told me about the military advantages, I visualized the slopes around Jerusalem, rich with olives and grapes.

"But," he continued, interrupting my reverie, "the most important thing of all: Jerusalem is neutral ground as far as the two Israelite parties are concerned."

"But Uriah," I questioned, "isn't David ahead of himself? Jerusalem isn't even under Israelite control but is occupied by the Jebusites."

"Not for long," he assured me. "The army under David is about to lay siege over Jerusalem."

Uriah's words became fact as he and his comrades made their way to Jerusalem.

He was elated upon his return. His face mirrored his excitement as he explained, "The siege began in earnest, but the Jebusites were very confident of survival and victory. They thought they were secure. So much so that they taunted David from the walls, yelling, 'You will not come in here. Even the blind and the lame will be able to ward you off.' Well, it turned out their deeds could not match their words. What they had in bravado, they lacked in military skill.

"Those silly Jebusites neglected to guard the tunnel and shaft that gave them access to water in times of siege." He laughed the joyful laugh of victory, as he told me how David directed a diversionary assault on the walls so that Joab and a hand-picked force could enter the water shaft and slip into the city.

"I was with Joab." Uriah beamed. "Victory was ours! The Jebusite city became the City of David!"

Jerusalem wasn't much of a city when we moved there. It covered only about eleven or twelve acres. And at most, there were only about twenty-five hundred people living here. Now, with my son Solomon on the throne, Jerusalem occupies at least thirty-two acres, and how the population has multiplied! We have at least forty-five hundred to five thousand people living here. And that doesn't even include the folks living in the surrounding areas beyond the city walls!

Do you know one of the first things David did when he had secured Jerusalem and made it the capital? He brought the Ark of the Covenant to the city. What rejoicing! I thought our wedding was a celebration. Nothing compared to the exuberant joy we had as we brought the Ark to its home at last!

I saw David—dancing and singing to Yahweh with all his might. How that man loved the Lord! He once told me that Yahweh called him "a man after God's own heart." But you may have heard that not everyone joined in David's exuberance.

"No," he told me later. "Michal, the wife that Saul had given me, did not rejoice with me. On the contrary, she called me shameless for my actions."

But it was our Lord God Yahweh who had orchestrated bringing the Ark to Jerusalem. Now it was not only the City of David—now Jerusalem was God's City—the Holy City.

I was so happy when Uriah and I made our home in Jerusalem. To be in the most exciting city, in such a lovely home! Ours was not simply a one-room house with a door and a gate, but a beautiful home with three—that's right—*three* rooms. You may know that the rooms in our homes are not built side by side as they are in your Western culture, but across from one another with a great open room between. No doubt you would call the open-air room a courtyard.

Ours was a spacious three-room house, each room facing an open courtyard. Can you picture it? One room was on the east, facing another on the west. Facing the room on the north was the courtyard wall. The courtyard itself was open to the sky, but we never considered it *outside* our home! It was part of the house. In fact, we had an awning over part of the courtyard, to protect us from the sun or rain. There were trees in our courtyard and shrubs and flowers. Benches were placed under the trees for our comfort, and a cistern for our convenience. The courtyard was one our favorite rooms. We spent many happy hours there.

But fighting men must go off to war. David always made relentless war on Israel's enemies. Uriah told me of the many battles, battles against the Philistines and the Amalekites. David and his army crushed the Edomites in the Valley of Salt. In a series of campaigns east of the Jordan, our fighting men subdued the Moabites and the Ammonites.

It was during the wars with the Ammonites that this whole thing started. I wept when Uriah went off the war. I never got used to it. But there was something peculiar about this war, something different. The king *always* went with his men to battle, but not this time. Strangely enough, he did not go with his army but stayed in Jerusalem.

It really gets warm (maybe hot is a better word) in Jerusalem in late springtime. That spring, when Uriah went off to war against the Ammonites, it seemed particularly uncomfortable. Thank God for the coolness of the courtyard. I spent many listless hours under the canopy, hoping for a breeze. Late one evening, when it would seem that all of Jerusalem slept, I prepared to bathe in the privacy of my courtyard. It was so refreshing to spend time in the coolness of the water. As I put on my robe and sandals, I heard a knock at the gate. Can you imagine my surprise when I learned that it was a messenger from King David's house? He wanted to see *me!*

You know what happened next! There I was—in what you might call a compromising situation—with none other than the King of Israel! That night is all a blur.

Oh, if only I hadn't been bathing that evening! If David hadn't awakened from his sleep and paced on the roof of his house! Why was he not at the front with his fighting men? I spent several anxious days and weeks.

And then—my fears were realized. I knew. I was pregnant. And King David was the father! My handmaiden delivered my note to David. It simply said, "I am with child."

The very next day King David's messenger arrived at my gate with a note assuring me that all would be well. "I have sent for Uriah. He will be home shortly." I read what David had penned, but more importantly, I understood the *unwritten* message. But in spite of David's assurance, I never saw Uriah again.

You may know what happened. The news spread through Jerusalem like wildfire. My Uriah died on the battlefield, cut down in the prime of his manhood. I couldn't believe it. I cried bitterly. The whole neighborhood knew I was in mourning. The death wail was sounded so that all of Jerusalem could mourn with me.

Relatives and friends continued their lamentations. I cried in anguish: "O Uriah, Uriah, my husband, my husband."

The professional mourners came to add to the death wail. They rent their garments to let everyone know how deep the grief was. At least two of the mourners beat their breasts to express their sorrow. In anguish I cried, "Rivers of waters run down mine eyes. . . ."[4]

And then the time of mourning was over. And David sent for me once again.

David's and my wedding was not like Uriah's and mine. But we were married, and I joined his other wives in the harem. Some months later, our son was born.

I still had not recovered from the birth of our son when I learned the awful truth—that David was responsible for the death of Uriah.

We stood there, Nathan the prophet and I, on the small balcony overlooking the courtyard. The words on the parchment sent a chill that dampened the afternoon sunshine. "How could he, Nathan?" I demanded. "How could he send Uriah into a battle he could not win, knowing he would be killed? Why?"

I read again the letter Nathan had unwittingly uncovered. "From David, your King, to Joab: See to it that you put Uriah in the hottest part of the battle. When he is there, pull back with the rest of the troops, and leave him there to die."

Nathan took my hands in his, his eyes mirroring anguish beyond belief. "David had a plan, Bathsheba," he explained. "He sent word for Uriah to come back to Jerusalem for a rest from the war. Then he *ordered* him to go home to be with you, to share your company and your bed. But Uriah would not. He felt it would be disloyal to his comrades still at the front in battle."

"O Uriah, Uriah. You died because of your valor." I cried until there were no more tears, the realization of my part in his death breaking my already bruised heart.

"The Lord was very displeased with what David did," Nathan said. "But David, a man after God's own heart, was called to task by Yahweh, and I was called to be God's spokesman."

Nathan could always gain an audience with the king. He was trusted and loved by David. So it was not unusual for Nathan to go to David.

"I have a story to tell you, King David," he began.

"Yes, Nathan?"

"There were two men in a certain town." Nathan began. "One was rich, and the other poor. The rich man owned many sheep and cattle. The poor man owned nothing but a little lamb he had worked very hard to buy. He raised that little lamb, and it grew up with his children. It ate from that man's own plate and drank from his cup. He cuddled it in his arms like a baby daughter. Then one day a guest arrived at the rich man's house. He had to prepare a meal for his guest. He needed a fine lamb. But instead of killing a lamb from his own flocks for food, he took the poor man's only lamb and roasted it and served it to his guest."

David was furious. "As surely as the Lord lives," he vowed, "any man who would do such a thing deserves to die! He *shall* die!"

David paced the tiled floor in his fervent anger. Nathan said nothing. The only sound was the movement of David's restless feet marching in time with his quickened heartbeat. Finally the cadence eased. It slowed. Then it stopped. David and Nathan stood silently, facing each other. Nathan looked deep into David's eyes.

"King David," he said, "*you* are that rich man! The Lord of Israel says, 'I made you king of Israel and saved you from the power of Saul. I gave you his palace and his wives and the kingdoms of Israel and Judah; and if that hadn't been enough, I would have given you much, much more. Why then have you despised and turned from the laws of God and done this horrible deed? For you, King David, have murdered Uriah and stolen his wife."

Nathan paused. Silence seemed to draw all the air from the room. "From this time on," Nathan told David, "the Lord has decreed that the sword will be a constant threat to your family because you have despised God by taking Uriah's wife to be your own. Because of what you have done, the Lord will cause your own household to rebel against you."

God, through Nathan, meted out the sentence.

David was appalled. "How could I?" He confessed, "I have sinned against God!"

David did not die for our sin—but *our son did.* My heart broke when I saw the lifeless body of my dear child! The tears made rivers down my cheeks. It was David who comforted me. His arms encircled me as he gently stroked my hair. Not a word was spoken, but I felt David's tears as they mingled with my own.

I discovered some small measure of why God so dearly loved his anointed king. David had a heart that could break. He had a soul that could repent. In those moments of anguish I learned repentance from a repentant king, David, my husband, and my king.

Nathan's prophecies came to pass. David's family was always to know trouble. People nowadays would say that ours was a dysfunctional family.

But God is so merciful, so faithful, he gave us another son. Less than a year after the death of our first son, Solomon was born. From before his birth, Solomon was ordained to follow his father to the throne of Israel.

Once again we had a visit from Nathan. "Hail, King David. Hail, Bathsheba. I bring you word from the Lord. Because of his mercy and favor, he has given Solomon an additional name. The Lord shall call Solomon Jedidiah, which means 'beloved of the Lord.'" Nathan was radiant as he announced, "Oh, how the Lord loves this child!"

And how we loved this child! What a joy he has been! We raised him to be a king, the heir to David's throne, the ruler of a great empire built by David's diplomacy and military prowess.

I often reflect on how different they were: the father from the son. David was a shepherd boy; he became a king with a heart. Solomon was a prince; he became an often aloof king. David was a poet; Solomon, a man of great wisdom. David united a nation; Solomon built the temple and palaces. God used both these unparalleled men to build his kingdom.

But alas, as David grew old, he became remote from the needs of our kingdom. He wasn't paying attention. Oh, how Solomon's half-brother, Absalom took advantage of the situation. He even tried to start a civil war. His desire was to be king, to displace his father, David. I don't know what would have happened to us if he had been successful. The outcome would have been very grim.

For four long years, Absalom plotted his revolt. He was handsome and personable. He almost succeeded in his plans to wrest control of Israel. It was awful. David finally arranged for all of us, family members and servants alike, to leave Jerusalem.

His words still ring in my ears: "We must flee at once, or it will be too late! Hurry! If we can get out of the city before Absalom arrives, both we and the city of Jerusalem will be spared from disaster!"

A flurry of anxious activity followed. We traveled light and as quickly as we could on foot. Our company included all the members of our household. When we reached the edge of the city we paused just long enough to allow David's troops to move past us so that they could lead the way. We made our weary way through the barren wilderness of Judah toward the fords of the Jordan near Jericho. It was good to see that David had not lost his touch.

He knew that we could cross the Jordan safely and continue north into Gilead, where people were still loyal to him. David was not giving up. "Military genius" was the title most often given to him. He had loyalists back home, too, keeping him informed, giving advice that would help us in that dark and perilous time.

What happened next was inevitable. The battle was unavoidable. Thinking back, it seemed a certainty that the conflict would result in Absalom's death. Absalom lost his life in battle, hung on a tree by his beautiful hair and run through by the sword of one of David's men.

David, who was acquainted with grief, rather than rejoicing at his enemy's death, mourned bitterly: "Absalom, O Absalom. Would that God would let me die rather than you! Absalom, O Absalom."

All of Israel mourned over the awful state of affairs. I had never seen David in such a state of utter depression. "O Lord," I cried in my own anguish. "Where are you? We need you."

Finally, Joab could hold his tongue no longer. With the courage of a man of valor, he went to David. I overheard his urgent pronouncement: "You have shamed all those brave men who have saved you and all your family. Your actions tell us that if Absalom were alive instead of dead, and if we were dead instead of alive, you would rejoice! Come, King David, arise. Go and speak to your servants. They need to hear a word of cheer and encouragement from you. If you don't go, then every man will leave you. Yes, this very night, you will be left alone, and who knows what evil will befall you, your household, and all of Israel?"

Even in his grief, David knew good advice when he heard it. He did as Joab advised, and his rule was restored.

But with the passage of time, David's health failed. Nathan and I were concerned to see his ability to govern become increasingly impaired. The question of a successor became critical. With that in mind, Nathan requested we meet.

"You look so distraught, Nathan," I said as we conferred.

"Haven't you heard the latest?" he said. "Haven't you heard that that schemer, Adonijah, has declared himself king? David doesn't even know it! It's not surprising that Adonijah thinks *he* should be heir to the throne. After all, he is David's oldest surviving son. 'I will be king!' he has said. And that schemer has his backers, you can be sure!"

I was horrified. "What? How can this be?"

Nathan had a plan. "Bathsheba," he said, "you must act quickly and decisively, so that you may save your own life and the life of your son, Solomon."

"What, Nathan, what can I do?"

"Go to King David at once. Do you remember that he swore to you that Solomon should reign after him? Remind David that he promised that Solomon would sit on his throne!"

"Yes," I said, feeling a weight lifting. It was clear that Nathan's reminder was right and his advice was sound.

"Why didn't I think of that?" I mused, remembering a long-past conversation I had had with the king.

I wasted no time in going to David. My husband's room was shrouded in darkness, for he was not well. Even before my eyes had fully adjusted to the gloom, I bowed low before the ailing monarch.

"My lord," I said.

David raised his head ever so slightly. He managed a whispered question. "What is it you wish, Bathsheba?" He took a breath, then added, "What can I do for you?"

My words tumbled over each other in their haste. "My lord, you swore by the Lord your God to me, your maidservant, saying, 'Most assuredly Solomon your son shall reign after me.' You said, 'He shall sit on my throne.'"

David's eyes opened wider as my words spilled out. "And now, look, David, look at what's happening! Adonijah has become king, and you, my lord the king, don't even know about it!"

I went on to explain to David that Adonijah had sacrificed oxen and cattle and sheep in abundance. He had invited all the king's sons, the priests, and Joab, the commander of the army.

"But, David," I cried, "one important person was not invited. The uninvited was our son Solomon!"

Tears stung my eyes as I reminded David, "O king, the eyes of all Israel are on you. You and only you should tell the people who will sit on your throne after you. Otherwise, we can be certain of this: when you rest with your fathers, Solomon and I will be counted as offenders."

While I was still voicing my concerns, Nathan came into David's bedchamber. He reinforced everything I had said.

When Nathan had finished speaking, David called me to his side and took an oath. "As the Lord lives," he said, "the Lord who has redeemed my life from every distress, just as I swore to you by the Lord God of Israel, Solomon your son shall be king after me.

Solomon shall sit on my throne in my place. I shall certainly do it this very day!"

I felt a huge weight lifted from my breast. I could always trust David, for he trusted the Lord.

David was true to his word, and while he still lived, Solomon became king of Israel.

David had always treated me as someone special. So, too, our son Solomon always showed extraordinary respect for me. Solomon was the king over a powerful nation and a proud people. And yet, whenever I entered his throne room, he would rise to honor my presence. He honored me even further by providing a throne for me to sit at his right hand. Never had a king's mother been shown greater respect than Solomon afforded me.

My life in David's palace had its beginning in scandal. There is no denying that the beginning of our relationship was anything but auspicious. But here's the secret: if the Lord is in our hearts, and if we learn true repentance as David did, we can expect great things and God's special blessings. We just need to avoid the pitfalls and strive always to walk the path of the Lord. In that way, we too can become men and women after God's own heart.

NOTES

1. The story of David is told in 1 Samuel 16–31, 2 Samuel, and 1 Kings 1–2.

2. Psalm 144:12, King James Version

3. Genesis 24:60, King James Version

4. Psalm 119:136, King James Version

CHAPTER 5

Naomi–

The Road to Redemption

What's in a name? Elimelech, Mahlon, Chilion, Ruth, Boaz, Naomi. Ah, there's a name rich with meaning: Naomi. And the meaning, well, it really fits who I am. At least it did in the beginning. It's a name with a double meaning. Naomi means "my pleasure" or "pleasant," and really, my life was pleasant!

I was married to a fine man. My husband had a special name, too—Elimelech. Now, that's another grand old name by anyone's standards. It means "My God is King."

I'd known Elimelech all my life. Everyone in Bethlehem knew him. He was one of the pillars of our community.

Our life together did not begin in poverty, either—oh, no. Elimelech was from an ancient family in our hometown. Not only was it a family of long standing in Bethlehem, but it was also a family of no small means. Destitution and hardship were never considered, even as a possibility. Funny isn't it, when you have wealth, you have respect, too? I'm not saying it's right or it's wrong—it's just the way it is.

We had a very nice life, those first few years of our marriage. Within a year our first son was born. We named him Mahlon, for he was a frail little boy. A couple of years later, I learned that I was once again with child. We had hoped that our new baby would be stronger, but, alas, he seemed about as weak as Mahlon, so we named him Chilion. What they lacked in strength, they more than made up for in character. They were my darlings. Life was pleasant. Life was—Naomi.

Oh, to be sure there was always trouble up in the north country of our nation, but that seldom touched us in Bethlehem. Our village was surrounded by terraced slopes covered with vineyards and orchards that were alive with olive and fig trees. Wheat and barley flourished in the fields beyond those lush terraces.

I loved looking out on the hillsides beyond the fields. I'd watch the flocks and herds grazing lazily on warm spring days. Elimelech would come in from the fields late in the afternoon.

"Where are my little Mahlon and Chilion?" he would call as he neared our home. His life, too, was busy and fulfilled.

But storm clouds of adversity were looming on the horizon of our placid life. I had not noticed the diminishing larder in our barns. I was so busy with my household responsibilities that I overlooked the dryness of the fields and the sparseness of the fruit from the once-abundant orchard. My own private world was so full, so joyful, that I could not see beyond the "here and now" of my happy life. But it was all about to change.

"The beginning of the end," I called it. I had just pricked my finger on the loom and was patting it to stop the bleeding. Something caused me to look up. *What! I marveled. Elimelech coming in from the fields? But it's so early! Something is wrong!*

He didn't have that same strong stride. He didn't hold his head as high. He seemed bowed down by some huge burden.

"What's wrong?" I asked, Chilion clinging to my skirt.

I'd never seen Elimelech look so downcast. A chill encircled my apprehensive heart. He reached down and lifted our son, cradling him in his sun-browned arms. He seemed to be groping for just the right words. Finally he told me things I should have known but was too preoccupied to take note of.

"My dear Naomi, we must face some critical facts." I can still see the look of dread in his eyes as they met mine. "The crops aren't doing as well as they should." There was a reflective pause before he continued. "Naomi," he said at last, "they are failing. The barns are growing emptier by the day. And to make matters even worse, the

Midianite raids are becoming more frequent. And *nearer!* We cannot count on help from Gideon. He has his hands full up north. I don't know what will happen next. I fear it will not be good."

I had never known Elimelech to face such deep despair. It matched mine.

Everything that we feared came to pass. We were about to experience the most severe blow we could ever have imagined. You have heard the word that describes the horrible plight, but I doubt that you have ever experienced it. It produces such a devastating situation that, when faced with its horror, you no longer act, or even think, in ways in which you normally would. You become incapable of thinking in the same terms you had before. Survival and selfishness become key factors, not just for a few individuals, but for everyone. Life becomes a question of "how to." How to behave. How to think. How to *stay alive.*

One word brings the dread clearly to mind: *famine,* a six-letter word. Just a word. Or is it? Famine—something perhaps that happens to someone else, somewhere else. But when it happens to you, everything you once held dear begins to crumble. You begin to see an ugly side of yourself that you never knew was there. You ignore it, excuse it, but it will not go away. You try to wish it away, but that won't work either. It's there, deep within you. It haunts you, taunts you; it convicts you.

"Don't yell at me, Elimelech. I did *not* eat your bread! I didn't even *see* your bread! Say, where did you get it in the first place? Weren't you going to give any to me? And what about the boys? Do you want them to starve to death? Whatever happened to sharing, Elimelech?"

As our stomachs grew emptier, our tempers grew shorter, our concern more pointed. *Something had to be done!*

"We're leaving," Elimelech announced at last.

"But where?" I demanded. "Where can we go? It's no better up north, and you don't want to move in with your parents. Where *can* we go?"

Sarcasm laced Elimelech's words: "Haven't you ever heard of Moab?"

"Well, of course I have! I can even see it on a clear day!" I responded sharply. "But Moabites are *not* friends of Israelites."

"We can make it," my husband assured me. "I hear that the famine has not hit Moab. Look, Naomi," he said, pointing to the land he was describing. "See their lush fields?" His voice took on a kinder tone. "We can have a fresh start."

"I'm frightened, Elimelech," I stammered, fear clutching my very being. My husband tried to comfort me. "It'll just be for awhile, Naomi. We won't make it our permanent home. It's just a—a sojourn. We can come back when things get better here in Bethlehem. Besides," he continued, "we'll only go to the *fields* of Moab. We'll avoid their evil cities."

"But, *Moab*," I said, repulsed by its very name. "Their people there are so *different!* They are our enemies. They're strangers, aliens. They don't even know the Lord. They worship all sorts of foreign gods and—and—well, they just are not at all like Israelites!"

"What choice do we have, Naomi?" he demanded. "The Midianites have invaded from the north. And the Philistines are to the west. Our friends who tried to get to Egypt were attacked on the road. They never made it. *You* tell me, what else can we do? Where else can we go? Or, maybe you'd prefer that we stay here—and die!"

I was convinced. There was no other way. We had to provide for ourselves and our sons. I began packing almost immediately for the trip east.

Just for a time. A sojourn, that's all it is, I kept telling myself as we journeyed farther and farther away from the only home we'd ever known.

Just in the fields, we'll stay in the fields. We won't frequent the corrupt cities. We'll soon come back home. Hot tears stung my cheeks, but the rumble in my stomach told me why there was no turning back. We trudged the fifty miles to the land of the Moabites.

Elimelech was true to his word: we did avoid the cities. We did stay in the fields.

"It's going to be all right," he assured me, coming in from the field we had purchased. Even though frail, Mahlon and Chilion were a great help to their father in his vineyards and barley fields.

Elimelech was right. Things were going well. The thought of returning to Bethlehem held less and less appeal for either of us. We had built a good life for ourselves in Moab. The horror of famine was even fading into the dim past, an unreal memory in the face of all this abundance. As for the boys, they were growing up—too fast. They were beginning to think about marriage and families of their own.

The comeliness of the Moabite women appealed to them. There was no doubt, we had really settled into our life in Moab.

I must confess, by this time, I hardly ever thought of Yahweh, our Hebrew God. I guess if you worship a god—it doesn't matter what you call him—Asheroth, Dagon, Molech, Rimmon, or even Moab's very own special deity, Chemosh.[1] Oh yes, we did dabble a little, but we were never seriously religious. Maybe I should have been. I know now that it would have helped to have had a clearer understanding of Yahweh when I faced the next tragedy of my life—Elimelech's death.

I couldn't believe it. Elimelech, dead. *But you were so strong, so sturdy, like a great tree planted by a stream. You were my strength. And now, you are gone, forever, to rest with your fathers. How could you die and leave me in a foreign land with two sons? Elimelech, how could you?*

I turned to my sons then. They were all I had. But Mahlon and Chilion had grown up. They were no longer my little boys; they were men.

"It's time, Mahlon," I told him. "You should be married. You must have sons."[2]

After the usual meetings between Ruth's parents and me, the marriage was finally arranged. Ruth would leave her parents' home and be with us, forever my daughter.

I had never known anyone like Ruth before. She possessed such inner strength, and yet she was so gentle, sensitive. Her warm, brown eyes danced with good humor. I felt a deep peace in her presence. Ruth was all that any mother would desire for her son. Her beauty was more than her outward appearance, it was a radiance that glowed from within. This dear girl shown with an inner beauty, a spiritual beauty that I came to love. She was the daughter I had always longed for.

Not long after Mahlon and Ruth were wed, Chilion married Orpah. How good it is when a mother's sons have wives as industrious and sweet as my two daughters-in-law. To be sure, they were Moabites, but then, who's perfect?

Did you ever have the feeling that nothing could ever spoil your happiness? That's how it was then. There we were in Moab, with full, prosperous lives. Of course the ache in my heart for Elimelech never left me, yet there was a certain contentment because my sons had married well. However, my peace was not complete, for I had no grandchildren. I even found myself *praying* about it from time to time. It is a great dishonor, to have no grandsons, and neither of my daughters-in-law had any children, not even a daughter.

So I had those two aches in my tender heart: the death of my husband and the barrenness of my daughters-in-law. Still, everything else was going well. We were all living comfortably. And we always had plenty to eat. Who can complain? Not I. Not Naomi. Remember, my name means "pleasant" or, if you will, "pleasing."

But then, several years after we had settled in Moab, a monstrous plague swept through the countryside. It spread like wildfire, devouring everything in its murderous path, including Mahlon and Chilion. They both were overcome by its power and destruction.

Oh, Yahweh, please spare my sons.

Ruth and Orpah tirelessly tended to the needs of my sons, their husbands, but in the end the scepter of death prevailed. Both my sons followed their father in death ten short years after he died. I was crushed. I was numb with grief. I was angry and bitter. *This is more than I can bear.*

"I'm going home," I announced to Orpah one rainy afternoon some weeks after the mourning period had ended.

"But you are home," she insisted.

"No, Orpah. I'm going back to Bethlehem. I'm going home."

She threw her arms around my neck and began crying.

"Ruth," she called out, sobbing. "Come here. I have terrible news."

Ruth came running into the room, looking at both of us, concern etched around the corners of her eyes. "What is it?" she asked.

"I have decided that the time has come for me to go home," I told her. "I can't stay in Moab any longer. This land has claimed the lives of my husband and my two sons. Everywhere I look, every sound I hear, is a reminder of my great loss. I must go back to Bethlehem."

Tears and pleading saturated the following days as I prepared for the fifty-mile journey west, back to the place of my birth, back to Bethlehem. The sojourn in Moab was over. I was going home.

The girls came with me as we began our westward journey to Israel. After two days we saw the distant border that separated Moab and Israel. I stopped on the dusty path. Ruth and Orpah stopped, too. My heart was heavy with grief over the decision I had made.

"Ruth, Orpah," I said to my waiting daughters-in-law, "you were very dear to come this far with me. But now, you must go back. Go, each of you, to your own mothers' homes. I pray that God will deal as kindly with you as you have with me and my sons."

My voice sounded unreal as I went on: "May Yahweh grant that each of you have a fine home with a fine husband."

My arms encircled the women. I kissed them, tears stinging my cheeks. Our sobs choked our words as we tried to say goodbye.

"I can't go back!" Orpah insisted, "I'll come with you—to your people."

"No, no, my daughters, you cannot," I said emphatically. "Don't you understand? I'll never have more sons to be your husbands. I am too old. And even if I did have two baby sons, even right now, at this very moment, would you wait for them to grow up? Would you give up any chance at all to have husbands? No, my darling daughters. You must go home. My greatest grief is for you. How tragic that the hand of the Lord has gone out against *me* and hurt *you* so deeply." Oh, how our tears of grief watered the road of our sadness!

"Mother Naomi!" Orpah cried, "I'll miss you!" Tears dimmed her hazel eyes. She turned then, sobbing, and started the long walk back to her mother's home. All the while, Ruth kept clinging to me. She would not release her hold.

"See, Ruth," I said as I stroked the despairing young woman's hair. "See, your sister-in-law is going back. Back to her people and her gods. Go on, Ruth. If you hurry, you can catch up to her. You can go back together." I tried to sound cheerful.

"Don't say that!" Ruth cried. "Please, Mother Naomi, don't tell me to leave you. Don't tell me not to come with you." She was resolute as she vowed: "For wherever you go, I will go. Wherever you lodge, I will lodge. Your people will be my people. And your God will be my God. Where you die, I will die, and there I will be buried. May the Lord Yahweh punish me severely if I allow anything but death to separate us."

For the first time in my life, I was speechless. There was no convincing dear Ruth to turn back. *Ruth knows the Lord Yahweh!* I suddenly realized. *Maybe better than I!* Although my own faith had been superficial, Ruth not only learned about Yahweh with her inquiring mind but had come to know him with her quick spirit. Nothing got past Ruth.

On we went, mile after weary mile. The way was made so much easier for me because dear Ruth was at my side. I was not alone. Still, the journey was arduous. But at last I saw the gentle slopes surrounding Bethlehem with their lush olive and fig trees. Bethlehem! Home!

"Look, Ruth," I said. "We are home at last!"

I really didn't expect such a commotion upon our arrival, but the whole town seemed excited and surprised to see me.

"Naomi!" one of the women called out. "Is it really you?"

I felt a new tinge of bitterness at the mention of my name. "Don't call me Naomi any more. My name now is Mara, for the Almighty has dealt very bitterly with me. I went away full—I return empty. Why call me Naomi, when the Lord has caused me to suffer so, and has sent such tragedy?"

I look back on that incident and I confess my unfaithfulness to the Lord. Surely he is the God of mercy, not of vindictiveness. Surely he is the God of all comfort. I thank him for the faith of dear Ruth in that dark hour.

We returned to Bethlehem in time for the harvest. Ruth and I settled down in our modest home to begin our new life.

"Thank the Lord," I said. "The harvest is bountiful this spring."

"Yes," Ruth agreed. "I noticed all the barley crops."

"And Ruth," I said, "one of the fields belongs to our relative, Boaz. He is a member of Elimelech's family. Boaz is not only a relative, he is a fine gentleman, a man of character, and a very kind person besides. It doesn't hurt, either," I added, "that Boaz is also a man of great wealth."

She thought a moment and then suggested: "Do you think it would be all right if I glean in his fields? We could certainly use the grain, and maybe we'll find favor with Boaz. Being kin, perhaps he'll look upon us kindly."

I never thought that I would encourage someone I love to glean a barley field, but the practice is common in Israel.

"Well, Daughter," I replied upon consideration, "the harvesters always leave ample grain for those without fields of their own. In that way, gleaners can follow behind them to take the grain that is left behind.

"Ruth," I sighed, "maybe it is not such a bad idea. Actually, there aren't too many options for a widow. This might be the best one. But stay only in Boaz's fields. Please don't wander into anyone else's. I wouldn't want anything to happen to you."

The next day, Ruth was up before dawn. We ate the bread that was left from supper the night before.

"Ruth," I said between bites, "let me tell you the way." I wanted to be certain that Ruth went to Boaz's field and to none other.

She listened quietly as I instructed her, and then she was gone. I spent an anxious day, awaiting the return of my darling Ruth. Long before I should have reasonably expected her, I began my lonely vigil. *Is that Ruth?* I wondered whenever I would see a woman approaching. *No, not yet.* But finally, it was Ruth! I recognized her graceful stride, even though burdened with much grain.

I ran to her aid. "Here, Ruth, let me help you!"

"What a day!" Ruth laughed, her weariness forgotten.

Our simple meal had long been ready and was waiting for us. But we were more eager to share the news of the day than the bread of supper.

"Come, Ruth," I urged. "Tell me about your day. Did you see Boaz? Did he speak to you? Come, tell me. What did he say? Do you like him?"

"Oh, yes, Mother Naomi. I did see him, and he did speak to me. I heard Boaz ask his reapers who I was. When they told him he came to talk with *me*. He knows that I am your beloved daughter-in-law and that we are kin. He said to me, 'Now, listen to me, Ruth, my daughter.' That's what he called me, 'Ruth, his daughter.' He said, 'You have to be careful. Don't go to glean in any other field. Don't even *leave* this one. Just stay close to my maidens. You just stay close behind the reapers. I have given them orders that they are not to bother you, in any way. And Ruth, when you're thirsty, you just go over to the water jars and help yourself.'"[3]

"Oh, Naomi," Ruth went on, "I was so moved that I bowed to the ground and said to him, 'Why do you even notice me? How is it that you are so kind to me, knowing that I am a foreigner?' And do you know what he said?" she asked. She did not wait for my response but went right on to say: "'All that you have done for your mother-in-law since Mahlon's death has been told to me. I know everything. I know that you left your mother and father and your native land to come to a people you didn't even know.'

"He told me that the Lord will reward me for what I have done. 'Yes,' he said. 'A full reward will be given to you by the Lord, the God of Israel, under whose wings you have come to take refuge!'"

Tears of joy found their way down my weathered cheeks.

Ruth took a breath and continued her tale: "I was so moved, dear Mother-in-law, that I was speechless, but when I finally found my tongue, I said, 'You are so gracious to me, my lord. You have comforted me and spoken so kindly to me, and I am not even one of your maidservants.'"

I had never seen Ruth so radiant or lovely. She was animated by all that had occurred that day. Boaz not only provided food and water for Ruth but offered her protection as well. I knew that he had to have been attracted to her grace and charm, but there was more. I was sure that he was equally impressed by her beauty and her sterling character. How could it be otherwise?

Boaz our relative, our kinsman. *Why, he can marry Ruth as her kinsman redeemer!* The realization was a ray of sunshine on a rain-swept day, dispelling many clouds of doubt. My cup of joy ran over, realizing that Ruth would continue to glean in Boaz' fields, day after glorious day. I was thrilled to watch their growing friendship.

Even in sleepy Bethlehem time moves on as, of course, it must. A tiny concern grew larger as the end of the harvest season neared. Although the relationship between Ruth and Boaz was sweet, it hadn't developed in the way I had hoped. *They really need to be married!* was the cry of my heart.

Threshing time had come, the time when the landowner and his workers spent their nights on the threshing floor. Why? Because of the dreaded Midianites. The memory of their long-established habit of confiscating the annual Bethlehem harvest was all too fresh. Those Midianites were a crafty lot. They would wait until the grain had all been threshed. Then they would attack. No wonder Boaz did not want to leave his crops unguarded. No wonder he slept on the threshing floor.

But this offered us a remarkable opportunity! This was the time that Ruth could appeal to Boaz. *Oh, if he will only marry her as her kinsman redeemer.* My heart burst with anticipation.

"Ruth," I called to her. "This is your hour, my dear. You must get ready. See, I have prepared your bath. And look. See what I have for you, a new dress." Ruth's eyes widened as I held up the blue vision for her inspection. "And Ruth," I continued, "I've been saving this perfume—just for you. Here, take these things. Hurry, get ready." I saw the bewilderment in Ruth's face. "You needn't worry," I assured her. "I'll tell you all that you must do."

I felt like a bride-to-be myself, no longer weary from the long day, but buoyant, ecstatic. Excitement grew within my spirit. My heart beat a crescendo of joyful anticipation as I waited for Ruth to complete her preparations. *I know she will be a vision of beauty,* I mused.

And at last, there she stood, more beautiful than I'd ever seen her. There was an aura of calm loveliness about her. She looked like a princess, her face aglow like polished ivory, her lithe figure displaying youth and charm. Her hair was soft as down and her smile spoke volumes of sweet promise. But all the lovely words one could utter would not adequately describe the unparalleled beauty that stood before me.

"Ruth, my daughter, you are a vision of loveliness." I took her hands in mine. "This is what you what you must do," I said. I instructed her in the acceptable procedure. When I finished, Ruth repeated all that I had said. I was assured that she understood what must be done. I embraced her. "Shalom, my dear. God go with you."

I spent a sleepless night. *Oh, Yahweh God. That you would grant my heart's desire for my sweet Ruth. Help her this night to find success in her mission. Help her to overcome any doubt or fear. Help her to feel your presence as she proceeds with what she must do.*

I prayed all through the starlit night. I would pace. Then I would lie down. Too anxious, I'd be up again. For a time, I sat at the open window, watching the moon cast eerie shadows on the house across the way. But, always—pacing, sitting, lying—my prayers were ceaseless. Finally, the first fingers of dawn made their feeble attempts to brighten the sky. And then, there she was, my darling Ruth, coming up the path from Boaz's fields and threshing floor. I couldn't wait! I ran to meet her! She was laden with six—that's right, six—full measures of barley.

"Ruth," I whispered, relieving her of her burden. "Hurry, my dear, let's go inside. You must tell me everything. You must tell me how you fared. Come."

The gentle light of early morning glowed softly on the wall above our crude table. We sat across from one another. Then she began.

"I went to the threshing site, Mother Naomi, just as you instructed. Boaz and his workers were having supper. *Will they never finish?* I thought anxiously. Little streams of doubt trickled into my consciousness as the time dragged on. Then, at last, one by one, the men took their leave. Only Boaz remained. *This is a mistake,* I pondered, as the moments ticked slowly away.

"Finally, after what seemed like an eternity, Boaz stood up. He stretched wearily and came into the granary where I had hidden. He yawned, rubbing his weary eyes. It had been a work-filled day. Then, at long last, he laid down, right next to a heap of grain."

Ruth looked out the window. "Boaz didn't have long to wait for sleep to overtake him. He pulled his blanket up around his ears and fell asleep. I listened to the sound of his steady breathing. I wanted to be sure that he was asleep. Ever so quietly, so softly, I lifted the cover from Boaz' feet. He continued to sleep, soundly, so just as you had told me, I laid down. For a long time I simply lay there, not even moving, holding my own breath, as I listened to the steady breathing of dear Boaz. And then, Mother Naomi, just about midnight—he woke up. His feet touched my arm as I lay there, quiet as a mouse.

"'Who are you?' he demanded. I was so startled, but I remembered what you had told me, so I said, 'I am Ruth, your maidservant. Spread your skirt over me, for you are next of kin.' I was not certain what to expect, but Boaz is such a gentle man! He spoke so tenderly. He said, 'May you be blessed by the Lord, Ruth.' He told me that this kindness was even greater than the first. He called me lovely and said that I could have shown my interest in young men instead, whether rich or poor.

"'Then he told me not to be afraid. 'I am going to do what you ask,' he said. He said that everyone in Bethlehem calls me a treasure—a true woman of worth. He agreed that he is a near kinsman, but he said that there is one even nearer, our *next* of kin.

"That worried me," Ruth said, but she went on: "Boaz told me to stay there all night. Then he said, 'First thing in the morning I'll talk to your next of kin. If he is willing to do his part, so be it. But if not, as the Lord lives, Ruth, I will do my part as next of kin.'

"So I lay there at his feet," Ruth said. "I stayed until morning, feeling an excitement, but there was anxiety, too. And then, right before dawn, Boaz filled my cloak with all this barley. I left the threshing floor and hurried home as fast as I could."

"Oh, my dear Ruth," I said, rising from my seat. I embraced my sweet girl, and whispered a thank you to Yahweh.

Ruth and I spent an anxious morning. We knew that Boaz was a man of his word, but what about our kinsman? Would he want Ruth for his wife? *O Lord, I implore you. I pray that Ruth and Boaz will be wed.*

Then, after an eternity of waiting, we saw a man approaching. As he drew closer, we knew who it was. "Boaz! It's Boaz!" Ruth exclaimed.

We sat on benches in the courtyard as Boaz related the events that had taken place. True to his word, Boaz had gone to the city gate where important business was transacted. "At last, our kinsman arrived," Boaz said. "I called out to him. 'I have a legal matter to discuss with you,' I said. He was curious, so he asked:

"'Yes, what is it, what do you want, Kinsman?' He knew, of course that a serious legal matter requires ten elders. I already had assembled them." The twinkle in Boaz's eyes danced mirthfully in the noonday sun.

He went on with his story: "When he saw that the witnesses were gathered to hear the matter, he said, 'Come, Boaz, what could be so serious?' That's when I told him about your piece of property, Naomi, and how you plan to sell it."

"But," I interrupted, "under law, it must stay within the family. Oh," I said, as Boaz' plan became clear, "our kinsman is the only qualified buyer."

"That's right," Boaz said. "And I told him that he had first choice. The deal seemed really good to him." Boaz cleared his throat. "That is," he said, "until he learned of the string attached. Ruth, you are that string. To buy that property, he would have to marry you."

Boaz beamed his delight. "I got exactly the response I had hoped for," he said. "My kinsman was adamant. He said, 'I can't redeem a Moabitess. Uh-uh, oh no. It would ruin my own inheritance. No, Boaz, I cannot do that. *You*—you, Boaz. Why don't *you* do it? Yes, that's it! *You* buy the property and marry the girl. Boaz, I hereby grant you the right of redemption.'"[4]

We laughed and cried together as we considered the events of the morning.

"We must make wedding plans, right away!" Boaz announced with glee. He shot a loving glance at Ruth as he and I began planning the event I had prayed for. What a time of joy!

Well, that was some time ago. The marriage did take place, the most beautiful I had ever known. Boaz, strong and sturdy, like an oak. Ruth, strong and supple, like a reed. *Thank you, Yahweh! You have restored my joy!* And now, I bask in the sunshine of their love. Oh yes, there was a son born of this union. His name is Obed.[5] At last, the Lord blessed me with a grandson.

Strange, isn't it? I learned about the Lord's redemption through the kindness and actions of Ruth, a "foreigner," who had no knowledge of Yahweh until *I* went to a foreign land. I was redeemed as well. I learned that *my* Kinsman-Redeemer is the Lord God Almighty.[6]

I was Naomi (pleasant) turned to Mara (bitter). But now I will forever be Naomi, because I have learned to truly worship. Oh, by the way, you may be interested in the meaning of my grandson's name. *Obed* means "worship," and worship of the One True God was the beginning of joy for me. It can be for you as well. May your life be *Naomi.*

NOTES

1. Asheroth, goddess of sensual love, maternity, and fertility; Dagon, the god of grain; Molech, detestable deity believed to be honored by the sacrifice of children; Rimmon, sun god of late summer; Chemosh, like Molech, also believed to be honored by the sacrifice of children by fire.

2. Sons were more highly prized in that culture.

3. It was not uncommon for gleaners to be abused by harvesters.

4. In that culture, if a man died, his widow married his younger brother. Their children would be considered the children of the brother who had died.

5. Obed became the father of Jesse, Jesse, the father of David.

6. A Christian's "Kinsman-Redeemer" is Jesus Christ, David's heir to Israel's throne.

Come! Meet Mary,

Mother of Our Lord

PROLOGUE

Some men are born to rule nations, others to be farmers or fisherman or carpenters. Some women are born to be queens, others to be bakers or maids or weavers. Some women are born to be—mothers.

Mother. What a gallant occupation. To mold the children with whom God has blessed you. It's awesome! *Mother.* That's all I ever wanted to be.

My dearest possession when I was a child was the rag doll *my* mother had fashioned for me when I was but an infant. It was with me always, while I was baking bread with Mama or fetching water from the village well or lying on my pallet in the corner of our one-room house in Nazareth.

I was born to be a mother.

As a young girl, I often prayed: "Oh, thank you, Yahweh, that I am betrothed to such a fine man. Joseph will be such a good father."

Yes, I was born to be a mother. But I never dreamed I would be the mother of . . .

Please don't think that I am mad. Hear me out before you make any decision about the things that happened to me, about how the

Lord performs his miracles. You see, I am Mary. And I am the mother of Jesus, our Messiah.

There, I said it, and you are still here! You have not bolted from the room in utter horror, offended that this lowly maiden from Nazareth would claim such an astonishing event. I don't blame you for having doubts. *I had doubts!* After all, I had never had a heavenly visitor before that special day, that day which is etched forever in my heart.

It had been quite an ordinary day, with all the ordinary tasks. I was just about to light the candles at dusk when I felt a presence in the house with me. *Have Mama and Papa returned from their visit with Joseph's family already?* I turned to greet them. But it was not Mama and Papa. No! It was this incredible being. He looked like a man, and yet he did not. When he spoke, he sounded like a man, and yet he did not.

"Rejoice, highly favored one," he announced. "The Lord is with you."[1]

Can you imagine how frightened I was by his presence and how confused by his words? *What could he mean?* I wondered.

He spoke in a kindly voice, allaying my fears. "Mary," he said, "don't be afraid. I am God's messenger, his angel. God sends this message: He is going to wonderfully bless you. You are going to conceive a child, a son, and you are to name him Jesus. He will be very great. He will be called the Son of the Most High. And the Lord God will give him the throne of his father David. And furthermore, Mary, Jesus shall reign over Israel forever. His kingdom shall know no end."

I could scarcely believe my ears. I was shocked. "How can I have a baby?" I asked. "I'm not even married. I'm a virgin!"

I held my breath as the angel replied. I'll never forget his incredible words, each one bringing the news of God entering into this world in such a simple yet magnificent way—as a tiny baby.

"Mary," he said, sharing God's precious secret with me, "the Holy Spirit will come upon you. And the power of the Most High will overshadow you. So the Holy One to be born will be called the Son of God."

And then, as though he wanted to give me further proof of God's power, the angel added, "What's more, Mary, your cousin Elizabeth also has conceived. And this in her old age! People said she was barren, but she will bear a son. Elizabeth is already in her sixth month—for nothing is impossible with God!"

I was convinced. My heart of hearts told me that all the angel said was true. "I am the Lord's servant, his handmaiden," I told him.

"O Heavenly Messenger," I vowed, "I accept whatever the Lord wants of me."

I trembled ever so slightly as I added, "May everything you have told me come true."

And with that, the angel left.

I had always walked closely with my Lord. I learned his precepts at my mother's knee and my heart burned within me to feel his presence always. I had prayed that prayer many times, and now, his presence was indeed within me.

I must go see Elizabeth! But first, I must tell mother and father and Joseph the things that have happened.

Mother and Father were well respected in Nazareth. Everyone knew them and loved them. When I told them about the angel's visit and about the Holy Spirit . . . well, didn't *you* find it hard to believe? One thing was certain, however, they knew me and they knew my walk with the Lord. I pray they were as trusting as they were loving.

Now, *Joseph*—that was another matter. His face took on the color of ashes as I related all that had happened. He rose from his stool without a word and stared unseeing at the dusty street that fronted his carpenter shop.

"I won't let them hurt you," he said finally, still staring at the bustling avenue. "We'll simply break the engagement, quietly. That way there will be no stones thrown. I will not be forced to cast the first one at you, Mary!"

Somehow I found my way home, shrouded in a veil of tears. Yet, I had made my vow to the Lord. There was no turning back.

I found my strength in Yahweh's songbook, the psalms. "For you will light my lamp; the Lord my God will enlighten my darkness . . . For who is God, except the Lord? And who is a rock, except our God? It is God who arms me with strength, and makes my way perfect. He makes my feet like the feet of a deer, and sets me on my high places."[2]

Yes, the psalms and the angel reminded me that nothing is impossible with God.

How true that is! My Joseph was visited by the angel, too! While he slept, that gentle man had a dream. "Do not be afraid to go ahead with your marriage to Mary," the angel assured him. "For the child within her has been conceived by the Holy Spirit. Mary will have a son, Joseph, and you are to name him Jesus, for he will save his people from their sins!"

The angel went on to remind Joseph of the prophet's words: "Behold! The virgin shall conceive a child. She will give birth to a son, and he will be called Immanuel (God with us)."

And through the grace of God, this righteous man accepted the angel's explanation. He *knew* it was a message from the Lord! As soon as the dream ended, Joseph awakened and rushed to my side.

"Mary! Mary!" he shouted. "We'll be married right away. Forgive my doubts. I know you are innocent. I know you are pure. The angel has told me everything. You will honor me by marrying me. Permit me, Mary, to raise God's Son, Immanuel, as my own!"[3]

Oh, what sweet bliss! The Lord tests, and the Lord provides. "Oh, yes, my beloved," I said to Joseph. "But there is something I must do first. Please understand, Joseph, I must visit my cousin Elizabeth."

I told him the incredible news of her miraculous conception. Once again, Joseph displayed his marvelous good will and righteousness and agreed to the visit.

Elizabeth and her husband Zacharias lived in the hill country of Judea, but the hasty trip there was uneventful. I entered their home, unannounced. Elizabeth was at her loom, her back to the doorway.[4]

"Elizabeth," I said, overjoyed to see her.

She turned from her task, her eyes wide with astonishment. "Mary!" she said, almost shouting. "What joy! The baby leaped in my womb at the sound of your voice! Oh, Mary, you are blessed above all women. And your child is blessed. You are blessed because you believed that the Lord would do what he said. What an honor this is, that the mother of my Lord should visit me."

I burst into song at Elizabeth's greeting: "My soul magnifies the Lord. How I rejoice in God my Savior. For he took notice of the lowly state of his servant girl; and now, all generations will call me blessed. For our Lord, who is mighty, has done great things for me, and holy is his name. And his mercy is on all those who fear him, from generation to generation."

My visit with Elizabeth and Zacharias was one of joy and laughter. It was a respite from the storms that would encompass my heart as I learned firsthand of the sin and depravity that lurk in the souls of evil men.

Finally, Elizabeth's son, John, was born. He would later be called the Baptizer. It was he who would herald the coming of my son, Jesus.

"It is time for me to return to Nazareth," I announced shortly after the circumcision ceremony. "I am eager to begin my life as Joseph's wife." We said a tearful shalom as I set off on my journey home.

My husband and I lived together in our tiny one-room house. It was just around the corner from Joseph's carpentry shop. *What a godly man he is!* I often considered. For although we were married, he claimed none of his rights until after Jesus' birth.

We settled into a workday routine that was familiar to most of our friends in Nazareth. There were times, though, when Joseph and I would find time to walk the hillsides and see the magnificent snow-capped Mount Hermon, northward, beyond the rich plains, or we could take in the beauty of majestic Mount Carmel.

"Nazareth may not be important in the greater scheme of things," Joseph would say, scanning the scene around us, "but it is our home, and I find it beautiful!"

One chilly autumn day I returned from the marketplace, feeling very large and very pregnant. *It won't be long,* I told myself, feeling the life within me move perceptibly. I was replacing my coin bag in its niche in the wall when Joseph burst breathlessly into the house.

"What is it Joseph?" I asked.

"Mary," he said, trying to catch his breath. "We have to go to Bethlehem."

I could say nothing. *This is no time for a trip,* I reasoned. *My baby is due to be born within weeks, or even days.*

"What are you saying?" I finally managed.

Joseph led me to the stool near the open door, guiding me onto it. "There's nothing we can do, Mary," he said. "There has been a decree—straight from Caesar Augustus. His plan is that everyone throughout the Roman Empire should be registered. He has ordered a census."[5]

"But, Joseph, can't we be counted *here?*" I could feel the hot tears well up in my eyes.

"Oh, that we could," he sighed. "But, no. Everyone must go to the city of his family's origin. We have to go to Bethlehem, the City of David."

"I see," was all I could utter in tearful response.

Joseph raised my head tenderly with his work-worn hands and quoted the prophet Micah. "But you, O Bethlehem, though you are little among the thousands of Judean villages, yet you shall be the birthplace of my King, the One to be ruler in Israel, who is from ever-lasting to everlasting."[6]

"Yes," I said, feeling a surge of God-given strength. "Jesus will be born in Bethlehem. His birth there will fulfill the prophecy."

We spent the rest of the day packing and praying, praying and packing. We loaded the donkey the next morning and began the ninety-mile journey.

Sometimes I rode on our little donkey; at other times I walked alongside with Joseph. The trip seemed longer than the five days that it took. We traveled through Galilee, Samaria, and Idumea before we finally reached Judea.

"How much further must we go?" I asked Joseph as we passed through Jerusalem.

"We still have about four and one-half hard miles to go before we reach Bethlehem," Joseph answered, wrinkles of concern creasing his brow.

"There it is," Joseph said at last, pointing to the cluster of tiny houses. They looked like whitewashed boxes sitting on top of a low, steep ridge.

"It's so small," I said.

"Oh, yes," Joseph agreed, "but what a busy place. Caravans traveling to and from Egypt often stop here. Bethlehem's caravansary was actually built in King David's time.

"And see, over there," he said pointing to the valley just below the town, "There's the field of Boaz. Ruth's tomb is right here, in Bethlehem itself."

As we passed through the entrance of the town we saw the Roman sentries. We could hear the noisy confusion of a city bursting at its seams. The marketplace was jammed with so many different people: soldiers and officials, wealthy Hebrews from everywhere: Egypt, Greece, even Rome. We even saw some aristocratic families from

Jerusalem. And there were people like Joseph and me, peasants and craftsmen from Judea, Perea, and our home province of Galilee. I had never seen so many merchants, all hawking their wares.

"There is the caravansary," Joseph said, pointing to the inn that stood at the edge of the square. It was bustling with activity. The courtyard was crowded with men unsaddling their camels and donkeys. They were already bedding them down for the night. Upstairs, the rooms were full to overflowing with weary travelers.

"Look, Joseph," I said, directing his attention to the flat roof. "Why, it too is completely occupied."

"We won't find lodging there," Joseph said, trying to keep his disappointment from his voice.

I knew he was right, and I was uneasy. I hadn't told Joseph that I was beginning to feel the discomfort that told me my baby would be born—*soon*.[7]

"You wait here, Mary," Joseph said, taking the coin bag with him. "I'm going to make a few inquiries. Maybe we can find lodging in someone's home." He squeezed my hand before he went on, disappearing in a swell of humanity. It seemed like an eternity until he returned.

"Nothing. Every nook and cranny is already occupied," he said, just as I felt a sharp labor pain in my abdomen.

"I'm frightened, Joseph," I said, close to tears.

"The Lord will provide," he assured me.

"Yes, indeed, the Lord *will* provide," a smiling stranger echoed.

"What?" Joseph said in surprise as we turned to look at the man who had overheard our brief conversation.

"Come," he said, beckoning. "There are caves in the hillside just beyond the village. The local herdsmen use them as stables. Maybe Yahweh will have one—just for you!"

It was a struggle to follow him up the hillside. I no longer walked alongside Joseph but rode the donkey, as my labor pains were becoming more intense and more frequent. I waited on my little mount as Joseph went with the villager to speak with the occupant of one of the caves.

What are they saying? I wondered. I knew they were talking about me and the urgency of my condition, for they frequently glanced in my direction.

At last Joseph began walking toward me with ever-hastening steps. By this time the night shadows had fallen. I could not see the expression on his face until he was at my side.

"It's all right, Mary," he assured me. "We can stay in this cave. The man who claims it as his own will leave his lamp, along with some clean straw. I looked inside. There's a feeding trough in the cave. I've put some clean straw in it. It's not the cradle I built for Jesus, but I'll make the manger into as nice a cradle for him as I can."

Tears stung my eyes. "Oh, Joseph, you are such a gentle, loving man. Thank you for your care and protection."

With those words still on my lips, another pain pierced my body, and another, and another.

Oblivious to the animal sounds and smells all around us, Joseph helped me to lie down on the bed of straw he had prepared for me.

The man from the village returned, followed by the midwife he had convinced to come to help. The night continued in a blur of pain. Finally, in the lantern's soft glow, the labor was over. The miracle of birth was accomplished. God's own Son was born.

Snugly wrapped in the strips of swaddling cloth, Jesus was placed in my waiting arms. The midwife's duties were over.

"He's beautiful," I whispered.

"Yes," Joseph said, stroking Jesus' tiny cheek.

We had our first visitors that very night. Of all the people in the area who could have come, it was the shepherds, whom we had passed earlier on the hillside, who arrived. Their appearance surprised me because shepherds were one of the least popular groups in Hebrew society. They rarely, if ever, went to temple. They were not versed in Scripture. Some people even said they were thieves. But they had seen the star.[8]

They tried to peer into the cave, but Joseph blocked their view as well as their entrance.

"Who are you? What do you want?" he demanded suspiciously.

"Oh, sir," the oldest of the group pleaded. "Please, may we come in to see the baby?" He pointed skyward. "See, there's his natal star. It means that the King is born. We have come to worship him."

Joseph was taken aback. "What makes you think that it is his natal star?" he asked the strangers.

"Why, the angel told us. Didn't you hear the joyous chorus from all the angels who joined him?"

"Yes," another shepherd added, "the earth trembled with their thunderous announcement!"

Scuffling feet. Pasture smells. Wide-eyed adoration. Sounds of breathing.

Kneeling men. Kneeling boys. Then, they were gone.

I pondered these things in my heart.

Joseph and I were always good Jews. All of our holy laws were observed: Jesus' circumcision, the purification, each at the prescribed time. Then it was time for Jesus' presentation at the temple.[9]

Simeon was there. I had never seen him before, nor have I seen him since, but the Holy Spirit came upon him when he saw Jesus. It made me think of my visit with Elizabeth.

The old man took Jesus from my arms. "All my life I have waited for the Messiah," he said. "The Holy Spirit revealed to me that I would not die until I saw him, God's anointed King. I have seen God's salvation in this tiny babe; he is a light to bring salvation to the Gentiles, and he is the glory of Israel."

Joseph and I stood in amazed silence as he said these things. Then he gave us his blessing. But a chill of dread filled me when he told me, "A sword shall pierce your soul, for this child shall be rejected by many in Israel. This will be their undoing. But he will be the greatest joy of many others. And the deepest thoughts of many hearts shall be revealed."

He gently returned Jesus to my eager arms, turned, and made his way up the temple steps.

Anna, the old prophetess, overheard Simeon's words. She too had been waiting for the Messiah to bring salvation to Israel. "I have longed for this all my life!" she said, tears of joy coursing down her ancient cheeks. With great joy she told everyone who would listen that the Messiah had been born.

I pondered these things in my heart.

We had many other visitors during our stay in Bethlehem, and among the most notable were the wise men, a band of scholars from the east. Like the shepherds, they had seen Jesus' star and had come to worship him.[10]

Scuffling feet. The fragrance of frankincense and myrrh. The warm glow of gold.

Wide-eyed adoration. Sounds of breathing. Kneeling men.
Then, they were gone.
I pondered these things in my heart.

"Mary, Mary," Joseph announced early the next morning. "We must flee!"[11]

"What? Why?"

"Herod knows about Jesus! He plans to kill him!"

"How do you know?"

"The angel. He came with a warning."

We fled to Egypt. An arduous journey. But, because of the costly gifts the wise men had given, we were able to make the trip and sustain ourselves until wicked King Herod was dead.

"Oh, yes," a friend assured us. "The old tyrant is dead. Dead as a camel at sea. He died in agony, old Herod did, his mind and his body wracked by disease. Even now, the rejoicing continues. No one mourned that evil jackal."

Joseph and I lost no time preparing for our trip home. Home to Nazareth, at long last.

"I thought this day would never come!" I told Joseph. "It has been hard, being exiled in Egypt. I've missed our home, our friends."[12]

"Yes," Joseph agreed. "But remember, the Scripture says: 'Out of Egypt I shall call my Son.' Mary, Jesus is Yahweh's Son. He is being called out of Egypt to save his people."

I added Joseph's words to those I already pondered in my heart.

Home! Jesus saw Nazareth for the first time when he was a lad, no longer an infant. We came home in the spring when the fields of Galilee were covered with a fresh, fragrant mantle of wild flowers. The gentle hills were alive with flocks grazing contentedly near the grape arbors. Grain and olives and pomegranates were in abundance. What a homecoming!

It was peaceful, pastoral, the day we arrived. Ah, Nazareth, nestled in a nook in the hills at the northern edge of the fruitful Plain of Esdraelon. We saw the familiar sight of the square little houses all huddled together, as though conversing in happy gossip.

"Ah, Joseph," I said, noting the wonder in Jesus' eyes. "See how he drinks everything in as he views Nazareth for the first time!"

"Look," Jesus said, pointing excitedly to the top of the hill. "What is that?"

"That," said Joseph, a twinkle in his bright eyes, "is the synagogue. I am sure you will become well acquainted with that place and its function before too long." His hearty laughter echoed against the hills and lingered in my heart.

As we drew near, some of the townspeople came running to greet us. They embraced us in joyful reunion. More friends came. Soon, it seemed, the whole town surrounded us with jubilant shouts of "Welcome home at last. We thank Yahweh for your safe return to us. You've been gone too long. Welcome home!" It was a joyful homecoming.

We settled into our daily routine. It wasn't long before Joseph was busier than ever in his carpentry shop. My day was filled with the household chores every woman in Nazareth knew. Up at sunrise to prepare breakfast, usually curds and bread. After the meal, Joseph went off by himself.

"Come, Jesus," I would call after Joseph's departure. "We're off to the marketplace to buy the fruit and vegetables we'll need for the day."

It was so pleasant to meet my friends and their children. We spent some time visiting while the children played together. Before long, we filled our water jars and headed for our homes to continue the day's routine.

I baked bread every day, except for the Sabbath, of course. Jesus loved to watch me. I took unground barley from one of the large storage pots and ground the kernels between two millstones. I continued until the coarsely ground meal filled the bowl.

I poured some water into a smaller bowl and crumbled in a small piece of fermented dough I had saved from the day before.

"This dough is the leaven," I told him. "And a little bit goes a long way. It is enough for the day's bread."

Sometimes, for a special treat or on a feast day, I'd add a little mint or cumin or even cinnamon.

"Yum," Jesus would say. He watched intently as I'd mix the liquid with the meal and knead it in the special kneading trough.

"Mama," he asked, "why don't you bake the bread right away?"

"Because, my child, it needs to rise." He always *did* like that word: *rise*. There were many other chores, but you ladies, especially, know how busy we all are running our households. Your tasks and mine may be different, but our goals are the same: to love our husbands and to raise godly children. You may not need to do your own spinning and weaving or make curds from goat's milk, but you do all the things that make you the best wife and mother you can be.

Dinnertime was especially lovely in our simple home. While we ate, Joseph often recited the stories of our Hebrew ancestors. Jesus was ever attentive as his abba (daddy) would tell him of the duties required of every faithful Israelite. Joseph often spoke of the covenants God had made with his people. And then, toward evening, after our dinner, Joseph would go up to the synagogue.

"Can I go to synagogue, Abba?" Jesus would plead.

"Oh, yes, Jesus. Soon," Joseph would tell him. "You just need to be a bit older. Soon you will be old enough; then you can go, too."

Sabbath was special. On Friday night, Nazareth's cantor would make his way to the very top of the synagogue. At the appearance of the first evening star he announced the beginning of the Lord's day of rest with three sharp blasts of the shofar.

I had already completed my weekly chores. All three Sabbath meals were prepared. All the lamps were filled with olive oil and every jug was filled to the brim with freshly drawn water. Everything must be finished by sundown on Friday, the beginning of Sabbath. I looked about the Sabbath table, satisfied. *All is ready.* I thought with delight.

I always prepared special treats for the Sabbath in honor of the Lord. Sometimes we even feasted on a boiled chicken. But we always had a variety of vegetables. And for dessert we often had nuts or melons, for they were among our favorites.

Jesus, and later his brothers, James, Jude, Joses, and Simon, as well as his sisters, were all bathed and dressed in fresh, clean tunics.

And there was Joseph, more handsome than ever, the soil of toil washed away and replaced with the fresh scent of perfumed oil and a clean, sometimes new, tunic.

There was always a sense of Yahweh's presence on this day, which brought joy and thanksgiving to our hearts and home.

Time goes so quickly. Don't you agree? Before I was really ready for that reality, my sweet Jesus was six years old. Time to go to school. Early each morning, off he would go, on his way to the synagogue, which doubled as a schoolhouse during the week.

"Here, Little Lamb," I would tell him as he started off. "Here's your lunch."

"Thank you, Mama," he would say, taking the basket containing bread cakes and a small jug of wine mixed with honey.

Oh, how I missed him. We were always very close, and I treasured all our times together. Joseph told me that he, too, found great pleasure in Jesus. "He is a most extraordinary child," he often said.

"He learns so quickly," Joseph would say. "And he is always so agreeable."

"Yes," I agreed, adding, "and obedient. He is curious about everything."

"I know," Joseph laughed. "He sometimes asks questions I don't have answers for."

Jesus loved to play when he had free time. He and his brothers would often go to the field beyond Nazareth, running and playing tag among the wildflowers.

Jesus often went alone, to watch the shepherds on the hillside or the farmers in their fields.

In some ways, Jesus was like all my other children. But in many other ways, he was set apart. Many of our friends and neighbors thought it was because he was the oldest.

"He spends too much time with the rabbi," one of my dearest friends commented one day, just before Jesus' twelfth birthday. "You would think that austere man, with his long robe and longer beard, would frighten a twelve-year old," she continued.

"Now, Tabitha," I said to my friend. "It's not hurting the boy. Jesus' passion is the Scriptures. And it pleases the rabbi to have Jesus with him."

"It pleases the rabbi that *anyone* would want to be with him."

We both laughed at Tabitha's impulsive joke.

Jesus displayed an eager excitement as we prepared for our journey to Jerusalem. As it turned out, it was truly his journey into manhood. His excitement was contagious, and soon Joseph and I shared in the newness of Jesus' joy. All the arrangements had been made for the care of our other children during our absence. We were ready to go![13]

At sunrise, four days before the Passover, we made our way out of the village, and beyond the lush green hills of Galilee. We were on our way to the Holy City to celebrate the Passover. This was a momentous first for my holy child. His studies with Joseph and with the rabbi, his poring over the Scriptures on his own, had instilled in him the very heartbeat of Yahweh and the significance of the Passover.

"Mother," he said as we traveled through Samaria, "just think of Yahweh's divine grace and his deliverance of his people."

"Oh, yes, Jesus, the psalms say, 'Blessed be the Lord because he has heard the voice of my supplications!' He not only hears, but he answers. 'My heart trusted in him, and I am helped.'"[14]

Jesus went on: "'Therefore my heart greatly rejoices, and with my song I will praise him.'" His eyes brightened as he continued: "'The Lord is their strength, and he is the saving refuge of his anointed. Save your people, and bless your inheritance; shepherd them also, and bear them up forever.'"[15]

"Amen," I responded. My heart rejoiced saying, *This indeed is the Son of God.*

I pondered these things in my heart.

We joined other pilgrims, and along the way others joined us as the festive caravan made its way southeast toward the Holy City.

We passed through the prosperous city, Bethshan, located in a fertile, well-watered site where the Jezreel and Jordan valleys meet. Jesus' eyes widened as, for the first time in his life, he encountered the pagan culture of Greece and Rome. He recoiled at the colonnaded public buildings of pure white marble and the Roman-style marketplace with shops crowded beneath a stone archway. But most of all, he was dismayed at the sight of the huge stone temples to Roman gods. Rising above the city, Jesus saw the massive towers of the Roman garrison. This indeed, was a new world to him.

It was Joseph who assured Jesus that we would stay overnight in the Jewish quarter. But even there, the people spoke Greek rather than our native Aramaic.

"And they dress oddly," Jesus observed, for the tunics were replaced by Greek-style togas.

We continued early the next morning, traveling the highway along the western hills, a straight and level road. A little longer perhaps, but easier than the twisting, turning course along the Jordan River.

There were no towns along this way, only occasional stone fortresses manned by Herod Antipas' soldiers. We spent the night under the stars. Then, one more day of travel.

We spent the last night of our pilgrimage beneath the lush palm trees of the oasis of Jericho. In the morning we resumed our journey.

We made our way carefully up the steep, rugged limestone ridge that rose sharply through the Judean desert. The road, which was guarded by Roman watchtowers, was now crowded with other travelers. As we neared Jerusalem, the countryside changed from bleak desert to cultivated fields, vineyards, and olive groves. We rounded the curve at the southern foot of the Mount of Olives, and there it was—the Holy City!

My sweet Jesus had never seen such huge, awesome buildings.

"Look," Joseph said. "Look, Jesus, the Temple of Yahweh!"

It stood, massive and beautiful, all white and gold. It dominated everything in view.

We crossed the Kidron Brook and entered the city through the Golden Gate. Jesus was fascinated with the colorful scene: people from everywhere in strange costumes, speaking unfamiliar languages. He asked a million questions and made as many observations.

"Where will we stay?" he wanted to know.

"We'll stay with Jude, the baker," Joseph replied.

We rented a rooftop from the same dear people each year, always making the arrangements for the next year before leaving for home.

We made our way through the noisy, narrow, crowded streets.

"There it is," Joseph told Jesus. "The home of our friend, Jude, the baker."

We unpacked our things, settled in and then made our preparations for the Passover. I hurried to the nearby shops to buy the required wine and herbs. As soon as I returned to our rooftop quarters I began to prepare them for the meal.

While I busied myself with these tasks, my "men," Joseph and Jesus, did their own marketing—for a year-old male lamb.

"He must be perfect," Joseph reminded Jesus. "A lamb without spot or blemish."

Joseph told me that the crowds they encountered were so great that he and Jesus found themselves stopped in their tracks, unable to move forward or backward, to the left or to the right. Joseph told me how he clung tightly to Jesus. They, along with all the other anxious men, waited for the three silver trumpet blasts that would signal the beginning of the Passover sacrifices.

"At last our patience was rewarded!" Joseph said. "A great cheer rose from the crowd as the trumpet sound reverberated through the courtyard at precisely the ninth hour.

"Oh, how Jesus strained to see all that was happening," Joseph laughed. "After all," he said, "this is his first visit to the Holy City. His eyes widened at the sight of the solemn procession entering the upper courtyard."

"Oh, yes," Jesus added. "The whole procession was led by the high priest. What a magnificent blue robe he was wearing! Abba said it was his ceremonial robe. And we could hear the tinkling of the golden bells that were on the robe."

"What was on his head, Jesus?" Joseph prompted.

"A fine linen turban," Jesus answered. "It was all blue and was encircled by a golden crown with the inscription: 'Holy to the Lord'!"

Joseph told me how he pointed out the lesser priests who followed the high priest.

"Then came the Levites," Jesus said.

"And then the temple officials," Joseph added.

"Best of all," Jesus said, "I liked the musicians playing their lyres for the all the marchers. Everyone in the procession was chanting the Hallel: 'O give thanks to the Lord, for he is good; for his steadfast love endures forever.'"[16]

Joseph went on to tell me that the sacrifices began when the high priest gave the signal. He said that as he and Jesus waited their turn, Jesus watched in wonder as each lamb was sacrificed on the altar, the blood collected in golden and silver trays.

"At last, our lamb was sacrificed, skinned, and dressed," Joseph said solemnly. "I was handed the lamb. At last it was ready to be prepared. I told Jesus that we must eat the lamb during the sacred meal," Joseph added.

"Yes," I agreed, as I lit the candles for our Passover meal.

During the meal, after the second glass of wine, Jesus turned to Joseph and asked the ritual question: "Why is this night different from all other nights?"

Joseph answered Jesus with a beautiful recitation of the miraculous story of the Lord's deliverance of Israel from Egypt. He continued with other stories of crisis and redemption throughout Israel's history.

"Oh, merciful Lord," Joseph prayed at the conclusion, "you have always been our strength and our shield, a very present help in trouble. Deliver us, I pray, from the slavery of our oppressors. Some trust in horses. Some in chariots. But, we, O Lord, put our trust in you. Amen."

It was no surprise that during the rest of our stay, Joseph and Jesus were frequent visitors at the temple. There was activity in the Court of Gentiles at almost any hour of the day. It was the gathering place for people to discuss religious or political questions, to exchange bits of news, or merely to pass the time of day. Many of Jerusalem's learned scribes came to teach or argue points of law.

"Abba," Jesus asked Joseph, "may I just stand over there, by the scribes? I want to listen to their teaching and debating. Perhaps they will allow me to speak." So it was that Jesus spent many hours listening to and even joining in the discussions of the most learned doctors of the law.

The time went by so quickly. Before we knew it, it was time to head for home. Our caravan started out early in the morning. After completing his responsibilities, Jesus turned his face toward the temple, to which he was so magnetically drawn. *One last look,* I thought, watching his resolute stride.

Joseph and I continued in a flurry of activity that did not seem to abate. And then all was ready and we were on our way, heading northwestward, toward home. "I will be so happy to get back to Nazareth, Joseph," I said. "I miss the rest of our children and the routine I know so well."

But soon I became uneasy. Where is Jesus? I wondered. I strained to see if he was walking ahead with the other children in our caravan. Once I thought I spotted him, but when I called his name, there was no response.

"Oh, Joseph," I said at last, "I haven't seen Jesus at all since we left Jerusalem. Where can he be?"

"Don't fret," Joseph consoled. "We'll find him. He's probably with relatives or maybe with some new friends he made while we were in Jerusalem. I'll look for him. Don't worry."

I watched as Joseph hurried toward the front of the caravan, stopping along the way to ask people if they had seen our son. The process was slow and painful to watch. Finally I could no longer bear just waiting, so I hurried to catch up with Joseph, wanting to be with him when he found our missing son.

"Is he with you, Abigail?"

"Simon, have you seen Jesus?"

"Is he with your son, Martha?"

The response was always the same: a sympathetic and emphatic no.

"Joseph!" I cried in anguish. "Jesus is nowhere to be found!" The heat of the afternoon sun beat mercilessly upon us as we exchanged worried glances.

"Mary," Joseph said, "we must go back-back to Jerusalem. If he is not here, well, he must be lost somewhere in the city."

"Yes," I said. "Let's go now. I will not sleep until we find our son!"

Without another word, we turned to make our way back to the Holy City to search for our boy. Still, we asked those we passed who were headed for Galilee: "Have you seen Jesus?" And still the answer was the same: "No."

Making our way back to Jerusalem was made more difficult because everyone else seemed to be leaving the city. Though the way was not easy, our resolve did not waver. For three days we swam upstream against the human tide-undaunted, unswerving, unwavering. We could not rest until Jesus was with us.

At last we were at the city gates. Although our search was hardly begun, we felt a certain relief because this was the last place we had seen our son.

"Let's go to Jude," Joseph suggested. "Perhaps he has seen him."

Once again, we traveled the narrow streets to our friend's home, but the festive mood was missing. Our only thought was to be reunited safely with Jesus.

"No, Joseph," Jude said, his face mirroring our concern. "Jesus is not here. I haven't seen him since the day you left. Then I think he was headed for the temple."

"That's right," I remembered. "He went there as we were preparing to leave. Hurry, Joseph. Maybe someone there has seen him!"

The crowded streets hindered the haste we felt in our hearts, but we hurried as quickly as possible to the temple. At last we neared the massive structure, making our way to the Court of Gentiles.

"There!" Joseph pointed hopefully. "There's a group of men. They look like scholars."

"Oh, I pray they have seen Jesus!" I cried as we ran up the steps.

As we neared the circle of men, who were in earnest debate, I felt my heart quicken. The voice of one of the questioners sounded like the familiar voice of my son. Could it be? Oh, Yahweh, please! Let it be Jesus!

In a manner most unseemly for a woman, I rushed to the group and there he was, surrounded by the religious teachers of Jerusalem!

"Jesus!" I demanded. "Why have you done this thing to us? We have been so worried! We've been looking everywhere for you!"

He turned to look at me, surprise widening his dark eyes. He seemed taller, more mature. "Why have you been searching for me?" he asked. "I thought you would know that I must be at my Father's business."

I pondered these things in my heart.

The angel's visit so many years ago had set my life on a divine course. And now, this latest revelation gave my life a new dimension. Jesus now knew that he had a divine mission.

When did he know who his Father was? When did he realize that he was—born to die?

Simeon's words, "A sword shall pierce your soul," were fulfilled many times during Jesus' life, especially the last three years, his years of healing and teaching.

It was difficult to see that even his brothers and sisters rejected him. "We hear what the people are saying," they would sneer. "But, how can *Jesus* be the Messiah?"

"He blasphemes!" screamed the men in the synagogue. "He deserves to *die!*"

But Jesus did have his faithful followers. And no one could deny the miracles he performed.

I saw my Jesus with the little children, how he held them so tenderly, listening to them, blessing them. Why Jesus' very presence was a blessing! I saw it over and over again!

I did not always understand. *Why did Jesus have to die? Why would his own Father, Yahweh, allow this unspeakable thing?* But I heard Jesus say that he lay down his own life—in obedience to his Father.

I remember the Passover when Jesus was twelve years old. He and Joseph found a spotless lamb. That lamb was sacrificed in remembrance of God's divine redemption of his people from slavery in Egypt.

And my Jesus, *your* Jesus, was the pure and spotless Lamb of God who was sacrificed for God's divine redemption of his people from the slavery into which sin had ensnared all of us.

I gave temporal life to Jesus. He died and rose from the grave to give me eternal life. He who was my son has become my Savior.

Surely he has borne our griefs and carried our sorrows; yet we esteemed him stricken, smitten by God, and afflicted. But he was wounded for our transgressions, he was bruised for our iniquities; the chastisement for our peace was upon him, and by his stripes we are healed. All we like sheep have gone astray; we have turned, every one, to his own way; and the Lord has laid on him the iniquity of us all.[17]

Yes, I gave temporal life to Jesus. He died and rose from the grave to give me—to give you—eternal life. Thank God that he who was my son is now my Savior. Is he yours?

NOTES

1. See Luke 1:26–38 for the Gospel account.

2. Psalm 18:28,31–33, New King James Version

3. Matthew 1:19–25

4. Luke 1:39–80 (Mary's visit and the birth of John the Baptist)

5. Luke 2:1–5

6. Micah 5:2, paraphrased

7. Luke 2:6,7

8. Luke 2:8–20

9. Luke 2:21–52

10. Matthew 2:1–12

11. Matthew 2:13–18

12. Matthew 2:19–23

13. Luke 2:41–52

14. Psalm 28:6,7b, paraphrased

15. Psalm 28:7c–9, paraphrased

16. 1 Chronicles 16:34, New Revised Standard Version

17. Isaiah 53:4–6, New King James Version

CHAPTER 7

The Woman at the Well–

Encounter at Samaria

My name is important to me. I'm sure you'll agree that identity and name are closely linked. You may call me Asenath. If that *were* my name, I'd like to believe I was named after that beautiful Egyptian princess who married Joseph, patriarch of the coat-of-many-colors fame. I still haven't told you who I am, have I? Up until now I've been known simply as "the woman at the well."[1] Not a very significant title, but it *does* tell you who I am.

I'm from Sychar of Samaria, a ho-hum town if there ever was one. The only reason anyone ever heard of Sychar is because Jesus stopped there one day. Of course, Jacob's Well was not insignificant, nor was Shechem, the city a short distance from Sychar. Jacob's Well, Shechem, and Sychar were all in the shadow of Mount Gerizim, where we worshiped Yahweh.

That brings me to another point—the Jews! The Jews and their unrelenting prejudice against us Samaritans! No doubt you remember the Civil War—the war between the North and South. The South was Judah, the North, Israel. The split came when Solomon died. We Northerners sure were not going to let his son Rehoboam rule us.

Do you know what Rehoboam said shortly after he took the throne? He said, "You think my father made your burden heavy? Well, that was nothing compared to the burden I will lay upon you. You will think my father's chastisement of you with whips was easy compared to the scorpions I have for you!"[2]

Our people were not about to allow the weight of our burden be increased even more by that upstart Rehoboam. Not on your life! We had just about all we were willing to take. War was inevitable. The split was swift and complete. Israel became a nation in its own right, no longer united with proud—no, *arrogant*—Judea!

Of course we had our problems. Unfortunately, most of our rulers were less than stellar. In many cases, their lives on the throne were not very long. Zimri, for example, lasted only one week. Ironically, he was killed in a fire that he himself had set. It was plot upon plot, murder upon murder.

Our first king, Jeroboam, came up with what he thought was a brilliant idea; he deliberately set out to give us an identity totally separate and distinct from Judah. He said, "If these people go up to Jerusalem to offer their sacrifices in the house of the Lord, then their hearts will turn again . . . to Rehoboam, king of Judah."[3]

Jeroboam felt certain that if the people went to Jerusalem to worship, they'd be lured back to Judah. And the consequence: his own life would be in jeopardy. He was certain that he would be killed. So he revived the traditional sanctuaries at Bethel, near the southern border, and at Dan, way up north. He even went so far as to expel the priestly Levites. Then, to complete the separation from Judah, Jeroboam set up golden calves. After all, we humans need visual aids to worship, don't we?

Later on, Ahab's son, Omri, built our capital city, Samaria, hoping to give us a national pride totally distinct from Judah. It worked.

We have had quite a history. There have been five distinct occupations of our land, beginning with Israel, of course. But then, in 721 B.C., after ten years of intensive warfare, we were ruled and oppressed by Assyria. We were crushed, not only as a nation, but as a people. We were tyrannized by our harsh Assyrian masters. They had a unique method of breaking the spirits of their captives. They scattered us throughout the Assyrian kingdom. This accomplished, the Assyrians then brought people of other races to our land to dwell among those of us who were left behind. Those people brought their cultures and their idols with them.

What were we to do? There just were not that many of us Samaritans left in our land. So, we did the only thing we *could* do: we began to mingle with these people from Mesopotamia. We exchanged ideas. They embraced some of ours; we adopted some of theirs.

They seemed a decent enough lot, and really, was it so bad—worshiping their gods? After all, my people still worshiped Yahweh. You must have heard the saying: "You're all right, as long as you worship God." But, on reflection, I'd have to ponder: *which god?*

My people of the Northern Kingdom, the Samaritans, suffered horribly under the heel of the Assyrians, while the Judean's down south were still relatively free. While they were worshiping Yahweh in the temple in Jerusalem, we were left with nothing except the crude walls on the acropolis of our once beautiful city. I tell you, life can be very hard.

Assyrian rule lasted four hundred long years. Our problems were not over, however, not by a long shot, because when the Assyrians were finally defeated, we had the Babylonians to deal with.

Actually, the spiritual rift between north and south had become a chasm by that time. The Judeans were carried off to Babylon, but unlike we Samaritans they had the blessing of being allowed to stay within their own Hebrew community. They continued the practice Yahweh commanded of separation. Separation from what? Well, they frowned on intermarriages for one thing. God had commanded *that*. And they refused to worship any god except Yahweh. Come to think of it, their faith in Yahweh seemed to become stronger when they were away from Jerusalem and the temple, there in faraway Babylon.

So there's a little background on who I am as a Samaritan. But, what about me—the person? I have lived in Samaria all my life. I grew up headstrong and rebellious. I never had to look for trouble; it always seemed to find *me*. There was something missing in my life, a void that I could not explain. Maybe that's why I never seemed to fit in. There are those who might say that I have had a colorful life. But, quite honestly, it was just plain hard. And lonely. "How can that be," you might ask. I rarely lived alone. As a matter of fact, I had already had five husbands, and the day I met Jesus, I had a live-in boyfriend.

To say the least, the people of Sychar were uncomfortable with my presence in their tight little community. In fact, most of them avoided me. You would think I was a dreaded leper, crying, "Unclean! Unclean!" I certainly got tired of their stares and whispered innuendoes. Come to think of it, they didn't have to avoid me. I was a master at avoiding them.

One of my most difficult tasks was marketing, because I'd have to do that publicly. It didn't take me long, however, to learn the time of day when the square was least crowded. That's when I would go.

Avoiding people became an obsession with me. For example, *nobody* in Sychar would *ever* go to Jacob's Well at midday. "Why not?" you ask. The answer is very simple: the heat. The intense, sultry heat. The sun blazing in the midday sky was scorching hot, so hot that even the air, stirred by a passing breeze, burned like molten ashes from a overheated oven! But, you know, I preferred the relentless heat of the day to the unforgiving heat of my neighbors' vindictive stares. So, off I would trudge the weary half-mile to that ancient well.

The day I met Jesus began like all the days before, but it is so engraved in my mind that I can recall every moment of it. Even now, I can picture every detail. It's amazing! I was up before dawn to start the fire in the oven. Having no children, I gathered thorns and stubble for the fire myself. (You'd never catch the man I was living with doing women's work!) I would have preferred taking care of the thorn gathering the night before, but I had spent the evening mending my worn clothing. I remember that on the morning I met Jesus, I was able to gather enough stubble for two days. *That's good,* I reflected. *Now, I can avoid encountering my hateful neighbors at least one more time.*

I was very lonely. It's not easy, living without friends. I was an outcast, shunned by the other women of the village. I hated it, but that's the way it was, and there was no getting around that!

It was high noon. The streets were nearly empty. The dust was even beginning to settle as I picked up my water jugs and began my lonely way through the quiet streets. Sometimes I imagined I saw someone watching me through a distant window.

Busybodies! my mind screamed in response. But I never said anything. I always pretended that it didn't matter. I wasn't going to give them the satisfaction of knowing how very lonely and unhappy I was. *Who do they think they are anyway?* my weary heart demanded as I took step after weary step.

It wasn't long before I found myself on the outskirts of Sychar in the fiery heat of the noonday sun. The perspiration trickled down my forehead, making its way into my burning eyes. I blinked the sweat away and looked toward my destination, Jacob's Well.

I must be imagining it, I said to myself. *It looks like someone is sitting there, beside the well.* I drew closer and, sure enough, there was someone there. A man. I couldn't make out his features, but the way he was sitting made him appear very weary.

Well, who wouldn't be, I wondered, *out here, in this heat!* By that time, I had reached the well. I kept my eyes lowered. In a practiced manner, I stole a glance at him as I began to lower the bucket into the deep shaft.

I was startled to hear him speak: "Woman, will you give me a drink?"

I almost dropped the bucket! I could tell by his accent that he was a Jew! Now, you may not think that was significant, but let me tell you—for a Jew to speak to a Samaritan was unheard of! And a Samaritan *woman* on top of it! The Jews hated Samaritans. How can I impress on you the depth of that hatred? It was so profound, so deep-seated that they considered us to be turncoats, deserters. The Jews called us infidels. To them we were unclean, unfit.

Some Jews considered Samaritans to be less than human! After all, in their minds, we had abandoned the "true" faith. Jews never understood the how and why of our Baal worship. They never accepted our insistence that *we* had the true Scripture, nor did they agree that the only Scripture was the Torah.[4] While they were developing the Canon and creating synagogues, we were worshiping on Mount Gerizim.

So, you can imagine my astonishment that this Jew was here, in Samaria, at Jacob's Well, speaking to me, a Samaritan woman! I was filled with wonder and suspicion!

"Woman," he repeated, "will you give me a drink?" I couldn't help but notice the gentleness in his voice and manner.

I looked at him full in the face for the first time. His eyes seemed to pierce my very soul. *How could such an ordinary-looking man make such a deep impression on me?* I had to look away from his steady gaze. I turned my attention to my water jug.

"You're a Jew," I quipped, surprised at my sudden boldness. "I'm a Samaritan. And I'm a woman. How is it then, that you ask me for a drink?"

I looked away from the vessel and into his face once again. His gaze was intent. His words had the ring of authority as he answered, "If you only knew what a wonderful gift God has for you. And if you only knew who is asking you for a drink, you would have asked me and I would have given you *living* water."

What kind of nonsense is this? I thought to myself. *I've known a lot of men in my day, but this certainly is a new approach.*

"You don't even have a bucket!" I said scornfully. "Do you know how deep this well is? Well, I'll tell you how deep—*very* deep." I felt my heart pounding as I went on. "Where would *you* get this *living* water? And besides, are you greater than our ancestor Jacob? How can you offer better water than this, which he and his sons and cattle enjoyed?"

I took a breath at last, satisfied that I had responded appropriately to such a preposterous suggestion.

He was completely unruffled. I have never seen anyone with such composure. It was incredible. And so was his answer: "Whoever drinks *this* water," he said, pointing to the well, "will get thirsty again. But the water I give becomes a perpetual spring within you, watering you forever with eternal life."

I was beginning to be convinced. *Maybe this man has some secret power.* "Please, sir," I said in a less confrontational tone, "give me some of that water! Then I'll never be thirsty again, and I won't have to make this long trip out here to the well every day."

The heat continued to bear down on us as he said, "Go home and get your husband. Bring him back here with you."

My response was automatic: "I have no husband."

"That's right," he said with authority. "You *don't* have a husband. You spoke the truth when you said, 'I have no husband,' for you have had five husbands. And you're not even married to the man you're living with now!"

By the beard of Jacob! Who is this man? How could he know all about me? I hardly recognized my own voice as I said to him: "Sir, you must be a prophet."

I realized that the heat I was feeling did not come from the relentless sun. Rather it was the result of the strange conversation with the most remarkable man I had ever met. I had become acutely uncomfortable.

It's time to change the subject, I decided, so I said, "I have a question, sir. Could you tell me why you Jews insist that Jerusalem is the only true place of worship? We Samaritans feel we are right worshiping here where our ancestors worshiped. Why do you Jews think that Jerusalem is better than Mount Gerizim?"

His reply amazed me. "The time is coming when we will no longer be concerned about whether to worship the Father here or in Jerusalem. For it is not *where* we worship that counts, but *how.* In other words, *what* is our worship? Is it spiritual and real?"

His eyes pierced my soul as he continued: "True worshipers will worship the Father in spirit and in truth. Those are the people the Father wants to worship him."

He paused a moment, peering into my eyes as one would look into the eyes of an immature child. His voice softened as he continued: "But you Samaritans—you know so little about him, for salvation comes to the world through the Jews."

"I may not know a lot, but I know *something!*" I told him. "I know that the Messiah will come. And when he does come, he will explain everything to us."

"You're right!" His face lit up as he agreed. "And I who speak to you now—I am he! I am the Messiah."

My eyes widened in stunned amazement! I was speechless.

It was at that precise moment that several men joined us. "Ah," the Prophet said, rising to meet them. "Hail to you, my disciples."

"Ah, Rabbi Jesus," they said, "here you are."

They treat him with such respect, I marveled. *Could this be Jesus, the rabbi from Nazareth?*

Jesus of Nazareth! My heart pounding, I dropped my water jugs alongside the well. The heat of the day all but forgotten, I ran all the way back to Sychar. By the time I reached the village, the streets were beginning to fill with the townsfolk. The first person I reached was my neighbor, Lydia. "Come, Lydia, come with me to Jacob's Well. I met a man there who knew everything about me."

She looked at me in wonder. I never knew if her surprise was caused more by my news or by the fact that I dared to speak to her.

Lydia was convinced that this news must be of tremendous importance. Why else would I talk to her, rather than avoid her as I always had? But there I was, ignoring the villagers' cold stares, passionately spreading the news of the unlikely visitor at Jacob's Well.

I didn't wait for Lydia's response. I had to tell the others. *There are Saul and Simon and all the rest.* I shouted the news for all to hear. Soon others passed the word along. Then I shouted above the buzz of questioning neighbors: "People of Sychar! Can Jesus be the long-awaited Messiah? Can he? I must see!"

I turned on my heel and ran with renewed vigor back to the well. *Why, they're all following me!* I marveled. *They want to meet this man, too! They, too, must long for the Messiah!* We all scrambled, headlong, to the outskirts of town.

"There he is!" I shouted, pointing to Jesus, seated beside the well, his disciples on either side of him.

As we drew near we could hear his disciples urging him, "Come, Master, you must eat."

As I reached down for my abandoned water jugs, I heard his response: "I have food that you do not know about."

His disciples, watching me as I came closer, wondered aloud about Jesus' food.

"Did she or someone else bring him food?"

"I didn't see Jesus bring anything with him."

"Someone from Sychar must have brought him something to eat."

I was as astonished as they were when Jesus said: "My food, my nourishment comes from doing the will of God who sent me. I am nourished in finishing his work. Do you think," he asked them, "that the work of harvesting will not begin until the summer ends four months from now?"

He gestured toward me and all the others who surrounded Jacob's Well. "Look around you!" he insisted. "Vast fields of human souls are ripening right here, all around us. They are ready even now for reaping. The reapers will be paid good wages and will be gathering eternal souls into the granaries of heaven!"

A poignant smile brightened his sun-darkened face. "What joys await the sower and the reaper, both together! For it is time that one sows and someone else reaps. I sent you to reap where you did not sow. Others did the work, and you received the harvest."

I hung on every word. New vistas of spiritual understanding were opening up for me. I sensed that great mysteries were about to be revealed.

"Oh, Master," I implored, "please don't go—not just yet. Please stay. We are your harvest! If you linger awhile, you can help me, help us, to understand. Only you can lift the cloud that surrounds the great mysteries of which you speak!"

There was something so special, so appealing about Jesus that my neighbors joined me in persuading him to stay with us a while.

Our spirits quickened within us for those two glorious days of Jesus' stay in Sychar. To sit at his feet in rapt joy and attention was to experience heaven on earth. In the cool of the evening we sat in the shadow of Mount Gerizim. No one stayed behind in Sychar. All other sounds and senses disappeared in the wonder of those moments as we listened intently to every word that issued from Jesus' lips.

"Salvation comes to *all* who would believe in me," he taught. "Those who believe in me, who know me as Messiah, those who repent of their sins and worship God in spirit and in truth will be saved. You can have that living water of eternal life through my saving grace." He reminded us that it was through the Jewish race that all the nations of the world would be blessed.

We pleaded with him to remain with us. "No," he said. "I must leave. But remember always to worship God. Worship him in spirit and in truth."

"You know, Asenath," Lydia said, as we watched Jesus and his disciples leave, "now we here in Sychar believe, not just because of what you told us that first day he arrived. We believe because we have heard him for ourselves. Jesus is indeed the Messiah, the Savior of the world!"[5]

That was three years ago. And now for the rest of the story. My life has completely changed because of that miraculous day at Jacob's Well. My live-in boy friend is gone—at my insistence. I've asked God to forgive the evil in my life and for his help in turning my life around. I'm not the only one in Sychar who has changed. All those people who rushed to the well with me that day have changed lives—lives of peace and joy.

Our joy turned to overwhelming grief when we learned the events of that awful spring day, the day when Jesus, our Rabbi, was murdered! We did not want to believe the reports, but we could not ignore them.

"Oh, yes," Jude said. "It's all true. I saw the whole awful thing. And to think, they nailed him to a cross! There can be no crueler death!"

He shook his head in stunned disbelief as we mourned as we would for a lost brother.

"But Jesus did not stay in the tomb!" Jude announced. "Oh, no! He rose from the dead! Yes, the buzz is all over Jerusalem about the many people who have seen him since his crucifixion! There can be no denying it. Jesus, the Messiah, has risen from the dead."

The truth of all his magnificent teaching, there beside the well, in the shadow of Mount Gerizim, came to mind. *"Salvation is for those who believe. We worship the Father in spirit and in truth. I give you living water that wells up to eternal life."* Now I know that my Redeemer lives! And *I* live, eternally with Jesus, my Messiah!

Jesus, my Messiah, could be your Messiah too, and *you* could have the living water of eternal life as well! You too can have the peace and joy of his salvation, for he loves you and gave himself for you. Have *you* met him yet? I pray that you have. Come to the Well. Come to your Messiah.

NOTES

1. The Bible does not tell us the name of the woman at the well.

2. 1 Kings 12:14, paraphrased

3. 1 Kings 12:25–27, paraphrased

4. The Torah: the first five books of the Old Testament

5. The biblical account of the woman at the well can be found in John 4:1–42.

CHAPTER 8

Martha—

Touched by the Savior

I've heard about you. I believe we are kindred spirits. You always want to help, whether the project is large or small. I know that is true. You want everything to be done to perfection. So do I. When you have guests, everything must be served with beauty and grace. I would agree with that. Do you live by the motto, "A place for everything and everything in its place"?

I'm Martha, but most often I'm referred to as "Mary's sister." Well, that's all right. I *am* Mary's sister, and she is *mine*. Mary is the dearest sister who ever drew breath, although admittedly we've had our differences.

Mary and I live in the family home in Bethany, along with Lazarus, our brother. Bethany is a quiet little village. Actually, Jerusalem is only about a two-mile walk from our home if you go by way of the Mount of Olives. I can't think of that beautiful garden spot without remembering Jesus. How he loved the Mount of Olives with its quiet groves and simple splendor.

I often remind people that his triumphal entry into Jerusalem began in my hometown, Bethany. That day is deeply etched in my memory. The excitement of that day. The significance! But I'm getting ahead of myself. I thought you might be interested in what it's like, living in Bethany in the shadow of the Mount of Olives.

My life wasn't always easy I tell you, especially because so much responsibility fell on my shoulders as the oldest girl in the family. So much more was expected of me, by everyone, most of all by *me*.

I was only fourteen years old when I married my betrothed, Jason. What a God- fearing and sensitive man he was. Like Jesus, Jason was a carpenter. And also like Jesus, Jason had learned the trade from his father.

A rabbi once said, "He who does not teach his son a useful trade is bringing him up to be a thief." Jason was no thief. He was a respected, honorable man, loved by all who knew him. But sadly, Jason fell ill after we'd been married for only a year, and shortly after that my beloved died.

Immediately the announcement went out that my husband had gone to the bosom of his fathers. The family gathered and wept— loudly. The hired mourners came, too, and there was a long period of wailing and lamentation.

I wept as I watched the women cover Jason with spices and paste. These were tied to his body by layer after layer of white bandages. I knew that the paste would harden. It would saturate the bandages until a hard mold, like a cocoon, would form around and preserve my beloved's lifeless body. I placed the white linen cap on his head myself, and Mary positioned the bandage under his chin to hold his jaw in place.

Of course the burial had to take place quickly, because the heat would cause rapid decay. I thank our Lord that Jason did not die on the Sabbath, because the burial could not have taken place on that sacred day. I could not bear to watch as Jason was wrapped loosely in a linen cloth. He was carried solemnly to the burial cave on a wooden stretcher. Our family cave had been widened to allow easier access. Still, it was a difficult task, carrying Jason down the steep, narrow steps.

Inside the cave, beneath the earth, shelves had been provided for a last resting place for those who had died. When the shelves could hold no more bodies of our dear loved ones, their bones were carefully and reverently removed and gently placed into stone ossuaries. These jars were stored in a corner of the cave, so that the shelves could be used again and again.

The mourning and weeping grew louder, more intense, as the mouth of the cave was sealed. The disc-shaped stone ran in a deep, inclined groove dug in front of the cave. Some of our neighbors preferred large boulders to seal their burial caves. A boulder was forced into the access hole deep beneath the cave opening. There was no easy way to remove either the stone or the boulder.

Through tear-dimmed eyes I saw that the burial cave had been painted white. I knew this was to warn the living that the dead were entombed there. According to the Torah, we were forbidden to worship God after contact with a dead person, even a loved one, until after a stipulated waiting period, which no one defied.

The trauma of my loss was so intense that I hardly noticed the stones in our path as we made our way back to the home of my parents. I anticipated the customary prolonged period of grieving.

Mary held my hand, rubbing it affectionately. "Martha, Martha," she said. "You must eat something. You'll lose your strength. You must take care of yourself! We need you!" All the while Lazarus stood beside me, unable to speak because of his own grief for the loss of his friend, his "brother," as he often called Jason.

But life, as they say, must go on. We learn to pick up the pieces and carry on as best we can. Because I was now a widow, I had returned to live in my parents' home with them and Mary and Lazarus. It was providential that I did, because not long after that, both my mother and my father went the way of all flesh, joining our ancestors in the family tomb.

I prayed the psalmist's prayer: "The Lord is my light and my salvation, whom shall I fear? The Lord is the stronghold of my life; of whom shall I be afraid?"[1] But, if the truth were known, the future seemed very bleak at that time.

Fortunately we three, Mary, Lazarus, and I, were not left destitute. In fact, some people said that we were a family of means. We had a two-story house with a broad outer stairway that led to the large upper room. Oh, what a lovely garden we had, with a well-shaded court. The heat of summer is so oppressive in Bethany! We were blessed to have this place of haven and rest.

Rest! There wasn't a whole lot of time for that. The servants had to have direction at all times. I personally supervised all of the meals that were prepared in the courtyard over the open hearth. I enjoyed preparing meals. I did it well. And in all modesty I tell you that I had a reputation as a fine cook and, I might add, an extraordinary hostess.

Lazarus, Mary, and I were looked upon as pillars of hospitality in Bethany. I don't believe that any rabbi visiting our village, or even passing through for that matter, wanted to miss the opportunity of dining in our home. But of all the rabbis we entertained, we *did* have a favorite, Jesus, the renowned rabbi from Nazareth.

I can still remember our first meeting. Mary was so taken with him. "I have never met a more gentle man," she said, "a more charismatic man, a more thoughtful man."

"No," I added, "nor a wiser man."

Lazarus agreed. "Jesus of Nazareth," he said, "is a learned prophet. I'm proud to call him friend."

As winter approached, we hoped that our rabbi, our friend Jesus would be coming soon. We had heard that he planned to celebrate the Feast of Dedication in Jerusalem. Joyful anticipation filled our home and all who resided there.

"I pray he will stop here on the way," Mary ventured. That was all the encouragement I needed.

"We must get ready!" I announced, sending the servants into a flurry of activity. Mary helped, too, in her unhurried, calm way. Every nook and corner was swept and dusted as we prepared for the hoped-for visit of the Master.

"You know," I reminded Mary, "Jesus is so special, I just wonder if God sent him as an angel in disguise."

"You're right!" Mary said, beaming at me. "Remember Father Abraham?"

"Yes," Lazarus added, "and Gideon? They both had special angelic visits."

We continued in joyous anticipation of the visit of our "angel," Jesus. Still, it would be shameful to turn *anyone* away. After all, God had provided our people with care and protection, and we needed to extend that same care and protection to those under our roof. To be inhospitable was unthinkable; it was equated with rejection.

The three of us discussed the proper greeting we would give Jesus when he arrived. *Are we merely to gesture our greeting with a wave of the hand?* I wondered. But that seemed so cold. Perhaps we could say, "Peace be with you," to which Jesus would respond, "Peace be with this house." Mary reminded me (as if I needed a reminder) that a kiss on each cheek would be more formal. We didn't feel that our relationship warranted a mouth-to-mouth kiss.

"But Jesus is such an honored guest," Lazarus added, "that I think we should bow before him."

We agreed and went on with our preparations. We would begin the meal with a glass of wine, diluted with honey, of course.

"Where's the honey jar?" I demanded of our servant, Abby. As it turned out it was in its rightful place all along. I was so anxious that everything be just right that I had missed it.

After the wine we would have the main meal, the *cena*. There would be three trays, all beautifully decorated, just for Jesus. Besides that, we would have a grand array of fruit, all beautifully, perfectly, arranged.

The meal could not begin until the honored guest received the token meal. Lazarus would give the "token" to Jesus. He would dip a piece of bread into the savory food, and he himself would place it in Jesus' mouth. Yes, Jesus, as the most honored guest, would be given the morsel to begin the feast.

The cushions had to be placed around the low tables. Jesus, of course, would have the honored position on the right-hand side of Lazarus.

"Flowers!" I demanded. "Where are the flowers?"

The intensity of activity continued into the early afternoon. In the midst of all this organized chaos, Mary came running from the outer court. "He's here!" she announced with joy. "Rabbi Jesus is here! He's at the gate!"

Without a word I rushed to let in our most honored guest, pushing back a lock of hair as I went.

I opened the gate, Mary at my side, Lazarus coming up behind.

"Rejoice!" I managed.

"Peace be with you," Mary and Lazarus said, greeting Jesus together in one voice.

"And peace be with this house," Jesus responded, a radiant smile lighting his face.

He took Lazarus's shoulders in his strong hands and kissed both his cheeks in a formal greeting.

We all laughed and talked at once as we entered the courtyard. Abby had provided the best cushion for Jesus, as well as several others in strategic places all around the room. A basin of water was brought to Jesus. A servant washed his feet, drying them with a soft towel. Oil was gently poured on his head to refresh him from his journey.

"Would you please excuse me, Rabbi, as I see to the meal?" I asked, bowing before the Master. He smiled his dismissal.

As I hurried to the hearth, I noticed Mary pulling her cushion closer to Jesus. She sat at his feet. I felt a pang of envy. I wanted to be at Jesus' feet, too! But there was still so much to do! Besides the meal preparation, I had to be sure that the guest chamber was ready for Jesus. *Perhaps I could just go upstairs to check it out before the evening meal,* I thought.

One frustration after another plagued me as I heard bits and pieces of Jesus' teaching. "Think not," he said, "think not that I have come to abolish the law and the prophets; I have not come to abolish them but to fulfil them. Unless your righteousness exceeds that of the scribes and Pharisees, you will never enter the kingdom of heaven."[2]

How can that be? I wondered. As I mounted the stairs, I heard him say: "You are the salt of the earth . . . you are the light of the world. Let your light so shine before men, that they may see your good works and give glory to your Father who is in heaven."[3]

I reached the top of the stairs, looking down at the scene below. *I've got to hurry,* I told myself as I turned from my reverie and peered into the room. It appeared to have been duly prepared for Jesus.

I ran down the stairs to continue the meal preparation, pausing long enough to approach the Master. He stopped speaking. He looked up at me. Jesus' eyes met mine, and he gave me his full attention.

"Lord," I cried. "Don't you *care* that my sister has left me to serve alone? Tell her, please, tell her, to help me!" I could feel hot tears of frustration stinging my eyes, but I blinked them back.

"Martha, Martha," Jesus said, love and compassion in every word. "You are so anxious, so troubled about so many things. You want everything to be just right. You think that we need to have many courses for dinner. You are preparing an elaborate meal." Jesus paused, wanting my full attention now. "Martha, *one* dish would have been sufficient. One would be enough! Mary has discovered the one thing worth being concerned about—and I will not take it away from her!"[4]

There's a proverb that tells us that a blow from a friend is of far more value than a kiss from an enemy.[5] I knew that what Jesus said was true, even though it did hurt to face that reality.

I bowed before the Master and cut short the preparations for the meal, all the while reflecting on his words. *I need to rethink my priorities,* I pondered. *Yes,* I realized, *being busy* for Jesus *has far less value than spending time* with Jesus.

Unaccustomed peace filled my soul. I was subdued for the rest of the evening. I began to feel a new calm. "To thee I lift up my eyes, O thou who art enthroned in the heavens! Behold, as the eyes of servants look to the hand of their master, as the eyes of a maid to the hand of her mistress, so my eyes look to the Lord our God."[6]

Jesus stayed the night. The following morning as he left for Jerusalem, he put his hands on *my* shoulders and kissed *my* cheeks, first my right and then my left. What joy filled my heart!

"Peace be with you, Rabbi," I whispered.

"And peace be with you and with your house," he said, his tender eyes never leaving mine.

I watched as he and his disciples made their way toward the Mount of Olives. He had set his face to Jerusalem and would celebrate the Feast of Dedication there. I turned and went inside.

Mary and I had always been close, but the bond grew stronger. I became less anxious about things; Mary was more responsive to my needs. We became more than sisters. We became friends, friends in and through our Rabbi, Jesus.

Winter melted into spring and we looked forward to the Feasts of Springtime and to the greatest of all, Passover, the celebration of God's divine deliverance.

But, all was not well in our household, for Lazarus had grown lethargic. I knew that he wasn't feeling well, and finally Mary persuaded him to lie down and rest.

"It's not helping," Mary said.

"What's not helping?" I asked.

"The wine mixed with myrrh. I gave some to Lazarus. He's no better! He's just getting worse!"

I rose from my task. "We need Jesus. We've got to send for him," I told her. "He can make our brother well."

Jesus and his disciples were in Perea, just across the Jordan River. I quickly instructed Thaddeus, our servant, to go to the master. "Tell him his friend is desperately ill. Lazarus needs him!"

Thaddeus loved my brother deeply. He wasted no time going to our Lord. Before long Thaddeus returned. "When I delivered your message to Jesus," he told me, "he said that the purpose of Lazarus' illness was 'not unto death; it is for the glory of God, so that the Son of God may be glorified by means of it.'"[7]

But sorrow of sorrows, before Jesus arrived, my brother Lazarus died! I relived the grief of losing other loved ones to death: my husband, my mother, my father. And now—Lazarus! Oh, if only Jesus had been there!

Our friends in the village, the paid mourners, even many of the religious leaders from Jerusalem came to console Mary and me. Everyone had loved Lazarus.

I sat in the courtyard, weeping. Suddenly one of the village boys came running in, shouting breathlessly, "He's coming!"

"Who?" I sobbed. "Who's coming?"

"Why, Jesus!" he said. "He's coming up the road from Perea."

I dashed past the boy so fast, I nearly knocked him over. I ran down the dusty path. Mary stayed behind at the house. Then I saw him! Jesus! Coming toward me, his disciples at his heels.

"Oh, Master," I said, out of breath. "If only you had been here, my brother would not have died. And even now," I said with conviction, "it is not too late, for I know that whatever you ask of God, he will give you."

Jesus told me in quiet, measured words, "Your brother will rise again."

I looked into the Master's eyes through my tears and replied, "I *know* that he will rise again—in the resurrection at the last day."

Jesus took my hands in his and said: "*I am* the resurrection and the life. He who believes in me, though he die, yet shall he live. And whoever lives and believes in me shall never die.

"Martha," he asked, "do you believe this?"

Time stood still on that dusty road, the tears drying on my cheeks as I realized an eternal truth: Jesus, my Master, my Rabbi, was more than Master, more than Rabbi. Jesus was the Resurrection! Jesus was the Life!

"Yes, Lord," I answered in hushed reverence, barely above a whisper. "I believe that you are the Messiah, the Son of God. You are he who is coming into this world."

Reluctantly, I turned to go. "I'll bring Mary to you," I whispered.

I found her where I had left her, in the courtyard, surrounded by mourners. I called her aside. "Mary, dear sister," I whispered. "He is here. He wants to see you."

She knew I meant Jesus. I watched her as *she* ran, followed by all the mourners who thought she was returning to the tomb. Sobbing, Mary fell at the feet of the Master. I heard her as she cried, "Lord, Lord, if you had been here, my brother would not have died."

Mary's travail and mine greatly affected Jesus. "I am deeply moved in my Spirit," he said quietly. Then he asked, "Where have they laid him?"

The mourners and the religious leaders who had followed Mary replied, "Come, we'll show you." They led the way, stumbling in their haste.

A hush fell when we arrived at the tomb. I saw my Lord overcome with emotion. Great tears welled in his eyes. Jesus wept.

I could hear the religious leaders arguing about the Master's tears. One group was saying, "See, Jesus weeps. Oh, how he loved this man." But others said, "Come on, now. This fellow is the one who healed a blind man. You'd think he could have kept Lazarus from dying! No, he weeps for his failure!"

None of this was lost on Jesus. He heard them. "Roll away the stone!" he ordered with authority.

"Oh, Jesus," I said, "Lazarus has been dead for four days already. There will be an odor by this time."

His gaze turned from the stone to me. "Martha," he said patiently, "did I not tell you that if you believe you would see the glory of God?"

Those words of Jesus set the men laboring at their task. With great effort, they rolled away the stone.

Our Lord lifted his eyes to heaven and said, "Father, I thank you that you have heard me. I know that you always hear me. But Father, I have said this for the benefit of the people standing here, so that they may believe that you did indeed send me."

After he said this, he stooped to peer into the tomb. A moment passed. The world stood still. Then Jesus cried out with a voice like thunder, "Lazarus! Lazarus! Come out!"

I held my breath in anticipation. There wasn't a sound. Even the birds stopped their singing. The sound of the wind through the trees had ceased. The whole world seemed to be holding its collective breath.

And miracle of miracles, there he was! Lazarus! Coming out of the tomb, his hands and feet bound with the bandages, his face still wrapped with a cloth.

What a Savior! Even death had no power over him! "Unbind Lazarus!" he commanded. Everyone was speechless, but everyone was quick to obey.[8]

Many people who witnessed Jesus' miracle believed and later were among his followers. But there were others, those who did not follow Jesus.

"We must go to the authorities," I heard one of them say.

"Yes," a companion agreed. "They must be told what has happened. This is getting serious. Something must be done!"

So it was no surprise that the Master and his disciples did not remain with us in Bethany. "We must say shalom," Jesus told us. "To linger would be dangerous. The plots against us are increasing, intensifying. It is best that we remain out of sight. My disciples and I will go down to Ephraim at the edge of the wilderness."

The disciples agreed. Peter added, "You're right, Lord, we cannot stay here. Our enemies have already gone to Caiaphas, the high priest. They are afraid of you, Jesus, afraid of what your growing popularity will do to their power."

Our friend, Amos the tanner, had hurried back from Jerusalem, anxious to warn Jesus. "Peter is right, Master," he said. "I heard Caiaphas tell your accusers that they didn't understand what is 'necessary,' as he put it. 'You don't get it,' I heard him say. 'You don't understand at all. It is *necessary* that this one man, Jesus, should die for the people.'" The tanner said anxiously, "Jesus, Caiaphas said that if you do not die, the whole nation may perish!"

My heart froze in my breast. My knuckles turned white as I clutched my water jug. Jesus' enemies were more threatening than I had realized! And our home would be one of the first places Jesus' enemies would look for him.

The tanner left shortly after his report, heading back to Jerusalem. Jesus and his disciples left, too, their destination, Ephraim.[9]

Some events are so momentous that not a single detail is forgotten. That is how I remember the day of our Lord's return and the days following. It was just six days before the Passover. Mary and I had been busy cleaning the house in preparation for this holy event. I was immersed in the search for any errant yeast that might still be in the house, peering into the tiny crevices where it might be hiding.

I didn't hear him enter, but I felt his presence. Has that ever happened to you? Something tells you that you are not alone. You just feel it. I turned from my task, and there he was, framed in the sunlit doorway, his arms outstretched toward me.

"Martha," he said. The way he said my name made it sound like music.

"Master," I said, going to meet him, work forgotten. The Master was here. We made our way to the courtyard—and this time it was *I* sitting at his feet, hungering for every word that proceeded from his mouth, choosing the good portion that would not be taken from me.

I planned a light supper. There was a feeling of anticipation in the air. You know, a feeling that something is about to happen, but you just can't put your finger on it. Even the disciples were not their usual talkative selves.

Finally the men began taking their places on the cushions around the table, Jesus at Lazarus's right hand, the honored guest as always. Neighbors and friends gathered around to take part in this pre-Passover feast. The meal was about to begin. Abby and I began by bringing the wine mixed with honey.

Mary followed solemnly, carrying, of all things, a jar of costly perfume made from the essence of nard. We all watched in wonder as she approached the Master.

There was a holy hush in the house as my sister broke the seal on the jar. She began to wash Jesus' feet with the costly perfume. *Where is the towel?* I wondered. Mary had no towel. But she was able, more than able, to wipe our Lord's feet. In deep humility and solemnity, she wiped Jesus' feet—with her luxuriant ebony hair. The whole house was filled with the aromatic fragrance.

Judas Iscariot was the first to speak: "Mary! That perfume is worth a fortune! It should have been sold and the money given to the poor."

That Judas! I thought angrily. *He doesn't care a mite for the poor. He carries the disciples' money bag, and I wouldn't be at all surprised to learn that he dips his filthy fingers into it.*

Mary looked ashen at Judas' rebuke, but Jesus sprang quickly to her defense: "Leave her alone, Judas. Mary did this in preparation for my burial. The poor are always among us, but I won't be with you very long."[10]

Those words sent a cold chill to my heart. There was no mistaking the storm clouds that were gathering against the Master. His growing popularity was *good* news for the people, but *bad* news for the authorities. They considered Jesus a threat, a rival, and they wanted no rivals. The suppressed murmurs of discontent could be heard everywhere, even by those in power. They could not hide their fear of this growing threat to their position with the Romans. *What if there is an uprising? Will they blame Jesus?* I worried.

And I worried, too, about the stir caused by Jesus' miraculous raising of Lazarus. *Were they planning to murder both Jesus and my brother?* The thought sent shivers of dread fingering their way down my spine.

But we all tried to put these thoughts and fears aside and enjoy the evening that had been arranged to honor Jesus and his disciples. Musicians and poets shared their gifts with the assembled guests, fostering the mood of quiet joy. The psalms of redemption were sung in majestic worship.

O sing to the LORD a new song;
   sing to the LORD, all the earth!
Sing to the LORD, bless his name,
   tell of his salvation from day to day.
Declare his glory among the nations,
   his marvelous works among all the peoples!
For great is the LORD, and greatly to be praised,
   he is to be feared above all gods.[11]

Then, all too soon it seemed, it was time to retire. Jesus, wanting to spend the night with his disciples, said farewell with a kiss. He left with the twelve, to sleep under the stars. The day had ended with

Jesus' words still ringing in my ears: "I won't be with you very long."
It seemed so ominous, it frightened me. "Nothing must happen to my
Lord!" I said aloud. The sound of my voice startled me. But, alas, my
body cried for rest, and I gave in to it.

The next day's activities began before dawn. The overflow
Passover crowd from Jerusalem began stirring, causing a ripple of
murmurs and shuffling feet. The donkeys were braying before the
bird songs of morning. I rubbed my sleepy eyes to wakefulness and
went through the courtyard to the iron gate. As I flung it open, my
eyes were greeted by a sea of humanity, all moving about as one.

Many people removed their cloaks, throwing them onto the path.
Others tore low-hanging branches from the trees and spread them on
the ground. The excitement reached a fever pitch as they watched
for—for what? for whom?

Finally, above the din, I made out the words: "Messiah! The Savior! God bless the King of the Jews! Hail, Jesus of Nazareth, our
Savior, our Messiah! Hosanna! Blessed is he who comes in the name
of the Lord!"

By that time Mary and Lazarus had joined me, and together we
pushed through the jubilant crowd.

It was Lazarus who spotted him first. "There he is! There's Jesus!
He's riding on a young donkey."

I remembered the words of Zechariah: "Fear not, daughter of
Zion; behold, your king is coming, sitting on an ass's colt!"[12]

Were it not for the great crush of people, I would have fallen to my
knees in worship and adoration. But, we stood there, Mary, Lazarus,
and I, our shouts of joy mingled with the tumult of the cheering
crowd. Finally the last pilgrim hurried by, dust rising from his san-
daled feet. We went back inside, each of us deep in thought and
prayer as we pondered the strange events of recent days.

News travels fast in Judea, and we learned of Jesus' activities during that whole week. We were amazed and fearful that he mingled so
publicly and openly when the authorities opposed him so strongly.
But we were not surprised by the honesty and candor of his words.
We always knew that Jesus taught with authority. Did you hear
about how he overturned the moneychangers' tables in the temple?
What a commotion *that* caused!

With Passover week drawing to a close, Mary, Lazarus, and I joined the pilgrims on the way to Jerusalem. The joy of the occasion was marred by our concern for our beloved Rabbi. As we passed over the Mount of Olives an ominous feeling of dread overwhelmed me. The sky suddenly darkened. The darkness turned into the thick blackness of midnight, overshadowing the midday sun. As the gloom deepened, I groped for Lazarus's strong hand.

"Lazarus," I cried out in terror. "Where are you? I can't see you! Where's Mary?"

Somehow we found each other in the deepening darkness, a darkness so deep we could feel it. Clinging to one another, we moved cautiously until we found ourselves beneath a tree. We remained in the security of that leafy haven until the darkness finally lifted. But as soon as the sky began to lighten, we felt the earth shake beneath our feet!

Earthquake! The ground was swelling like a rolling wave on the Mediterranean Sea. My legs could no longer hold me. I fell like a limp doll, as did Mary. Only Lazarus remained erect. The tremor seemed to last forever, but as soon as it had begun, it was over.

"Let's go home!" Mary sobbed.

"No," Lazarus said tenderly. "The worst seems to be over. Let us go to the temple to sacrifice our Passover lamb."

The lamb! In the horror of the afternoon, I had forgotten all about the little creature, but there was Lazarus, still clinging to the frightened animal.

As we neared the city wall, the buzz of human voices echoed a chilling message.

Can it be true? I could not utter the words of terror that gripped my heart. But from everywhere, from everyone came the same message: "They have crucified him."

Finally Lazarus stopped a man to ask, "Who—who have they crucified?"

"Jesus," he answered.

"On what charge? What charge could they bring against him?" he asked.

"The charge? Simply this," he answered in astonishment. "'This is Jesus, the King of the Jews.' Can you believe that? Crucifying a man because he's a king!" And with that the man left, shaking his head in disbelief.

We continued on our way, feeling the weight of grief like nothing we had ever known before. *The Messiah, dead? Where is our hope?*

We reached the temple at last, but here, too, everything had taken on an unreal look and feel. Mary and I had planned to stay in the Court of Women while Lazarus went into the temple to sacrifice the lamb, but we followed him instead.

"You can't go in there!" the temple guard shouted at my brother.

"But I must sacrifice my lamb!" Lazarus insisted.

"I'm sorry," the guard explained. "There's been a terrible tragedy. The curtain to the Holy of Holies has been torn—from top to bottom!"

"What?" Lazarus said in horror. "How?"

"How?" the guard mocked. "How do I know how? All I know is that it happened during the crucifixion." He held his weapon to his chest and glared at us, his eyes telling us clearly his intention to prevent anyone's entry. The heavy doors were shut. We could not enter.

The afternoon shadows were lengthening. Soon it would be evening. It was nearly Shabat. We hurried to the home of Mark's mother. Perhaps we could spend the Sabbath there. We were not disappointed.

"Thank you for your gracious hospitality," I told her. "How has it been for you during this awful day?"

That was when she told us that Jesus and his disciples had eaten their Passover meal in her upper room.

"It was so unreal," she told us. "Not like any Passover I have ever known. Jesus began by washing his disciples' feet. Think of that humble task! But that's not all! I heard him say that the bread he broke was his body, that it was broken for them. And when he lifted the prophet's cup, Jesus said that the wine was his blood. He said: 'This wine is God's new covenant, new agreement to save you—an agreement sealed with the blood I will pour out to buy back your souls.'" [13]

Tears filled our friend's eyes when she told us of Judas' betrayal of our Lord. "Jesus called him 'friend,'" she said. "But Judas betrayed him—for thirty pieces of silver, the price of a slave."

I can't bear to relate the events that followed, but certainly you know. You must have heard what they did to my Lord, how they unjustly arrested him on trumped-up charges. Certainly you know how he suffered terrible cruelty at the hands of sinful men. My Lord deserved a wreath of gold, but he wore instead that awful crown of thorns.

Oh Jesus, what pain and degradation you suffered. Who has known such sorrow, such grief? And horror of horrors, the final insult, the final blow—the cross of Calvary!

How could they *not* have known who Jesus was? They crucified him. They murdered Jesus!

But not they alone. I had my part in it. Jesus said, "If you break *one* of God's laws, you have broken them *all*. Remember, all have sinned and come short of the glory of God!"

He died the most abominable death of a criminal, on the most shameful of all devices—the dreaded "tree." They laid my Savior in a tomb. They sealed it. We grieved. But the Son of God did not stay in the tomb. *No!* Death has no power over the Messiah. Jesus rose from the dead.

> He's gone, dear ones—no longer dead!
> He's risen from the grave!
> Death's no longer the victor,
> And we're no longer slaves.

> For Christ has kept his promise,
> To bring eternal life.
> Resurrection is accomplished,
> Turning darkness into light.

> Our hope now lies beyond the grave,
> For us, the "second-born."
> Jesus Christ did conquer death
> On that blessed Easter morn.
> Knowing Jesus Christ as Savior,
> Knowing him as Lord—
> Brings eternal blessings now
> And forevermore!

I know now that his death on the cross was in my place. I was well acquainted with my sinful self. Now I know his loving mercy. He who knew no sin became sin for me. He died so that I could live.

And his resurrection sealed my eternal life. He said, "I go to prepare a place for you, so that where I am, you may be also.

"If you believe in me, Martha, you shall live. Even though the body will die, your soul will live—with me—eternally in heaven, where a place is prepared for you. Believe in me and be saved. Believe and live."

Oh, Jesus, I do believe. And I love you even more now than I did when I first knew you in Bethany. All I can give you is my love and my self.

Thank you, Jesus! And thank you, reader, for allowing me to share my story. Remember me—when you get too busy.

NOTES

1. Psalm 27:1, New King James Version
2. Matthew 5:17, 20, Revised Standard Version
3. Matthew 5:13ff, Revised Standard Version
4. Luke 10:38–41, paraphrased
5. Proverbs 27:6, Revised Standard Version
6. Psalm 123:1,2, Revised Standard Version
7. John 11:4, Revised Standard Version
8. John 11:3–44, paraphrased
9. John 11:45–54, paraphrased
10. John 12:1–8, paraphrased
11. Psalm 96:1–4, Revised Standard Version
12. Zechariah 9:9, paraphrased
13. Luke 22:20, paraphrased

Priscilla—

Teacher, Preacher, and Tentmaker

My name is Priscilla, but my friends call me Prisca. Actually, it was Paul who first called me Prisca. An affectionate nickname, don't you think? Not everyone's name lends itself to a nickname. Take my husband, Aquila, for example. I tried to think of one for him, but for the life of me I could not come up with one that would be appropriate. The closest I came to selecting one I liked was Will, but, no, it just does not fit my dear husband. So Aquila he is, and Aquila he will remain.

But, after all, what's in a name? The real essence of a person is his or her character. And it is true that our experiences, and how we respond to them, help to mold our characters. As I relate some of my experiences and my responses, perhaps you will get to know me better.

I grew up in Rome, the most important city of my day. The magnificent city of beauty and culture was also a bedrock of religion. The Romans were very religious people. Even as a child I was aware of how broadminded and all-inclusive they were in their many-faceted religious tastes. In the early days of Roman history, religion centered in the home.[1] Granted, it was a very simple pattern of belief and worship, but it was strongly believed and practiced by most Roman citizens. Later, state gods developed. Each city or village had its own special god.

Janus began as the god of the family door sill, but eventually, he became the tremendously important and impressive two-faced deity of the gate to the Roman Forum, no less!

Vesta, the goddess of home and hearth, became the sacred state deity of fires. Her perpetual flame was kept burning by patrician vestal virgins.

When I was a girl, emperor worship was popular. It was strongly believed that the emperor was a god, especially by the emperor himself. Still, the Romans did not object to the rise of the many mystery cults. Remember, the Romans were extremely religious as well as broadminded. Regarding the numerous mystery cults of the time, the famed philosopher Cicero said, "A man cannot but be nobler for beholding them."

One of the mystery cults that developed was that strange religion called Christianity. But, as a good Jew, I didn't bother much about it. On the other hand, Aquila, my husband, showed some interest. He was more adventurous than I. His adventuresome nature prompted him to leave his home in Pontus overlooking the Black Sea to journey the long distance through mountains and over seas to come to Rome.

"Why come all this way, Aquila?" I asked one Sabbath evening.

"Rome is the center of everything," he said, "including commerce. I left my tent-making business in Pontus to start fresh here. And with Yahweh's help, I shall succeed."

I had never met anyone from Asia Minor before and was fascinated as he told stories about the archaic way of life in that rugged outpost of civilization. I was surprised to learn that there was a Jewish community in that faraway, primitive place.

"The natives of the land are just as rough as the terrain," Aquila explained, "rough and tumble." *Why would any Jew want to stay in a place like that?* I wondered.

"I *never* want to leave my beloved Rome," I responded.

"Nor do I," he agreed. "Not only is business prosperous, but more important, dear Priscilla, this is where I found you!"

Aquila was embracing Roman life. He not only adopted Rome's ways but also married one of her daughters—me!

That Aquila—what a businessman! In no time at all he had established himself as one of the leading tentmakers in all of Rome.

"I am so glad you hired people to do the leather work out of town and downwind!" I told him one day. "Phew! I love working with you, but that is one part of the operation I want nothing to do with."

Aquila laughed at my wrinkled-up nose as he explained the procedure. "First of all," he said, "Cornelius, our leather worker, must skin the animal. Then he carefully removes all the hairs from the hide."

"I know," I interrupted. "And I've seen how he works the hide after all the hairs are gone. There is no stopping him until the skin is soft and supple. He puts everything he has into the task as he scrapes, soaks, and applies the lime."

It was Aquila's turn to interrupt. "That's only the beginning. Then, Cornelius has to soak the hides in water containing oak galls and sumac leaves." He cleared his throat before continuing. "Do you know what's next?" he asked, a twinkle in his eye.

"Oh, yes," I said. "That's why I am so glad that he works downwind!" I took a deep breath before continuing, then said, "He rubs the hide with, of all things, dog manure! Yuck!"

Aquila laughed till the tears of mirth ran down his tan cheeks.

"Enough frivolity!" I announced. "It's time for *us* to get back to work." Aquila and I did the more creative, less offensive, work in our shop in Rome.

We had settled into a very happy routine. It was not all work and no play—not for Aquila and Priscilla! We entertained frequently. Our home was spacious, and hospitality was the byword of the day. Feasts and intimate dinners were not at all unusual in our home.

Many an evening was spent with friends, debating such questions as:
"Who is a true Jew?"
"What does God require of his people?"
"What is the destiny of Israel?"
Those debates were important, not only for their conversational value but for our broadened understanding of our heritage as Jews, God's chosen people.

Aquila, and all our friends for that matter, had a great interest in tracing our lineage. Sometimes it was to identify ourselves with well-known priests. Sometimes it helped to establish our family roots. But for Aquila and me, the burning desire was to identify ourselves with the promised Messiah.

All too soon, however, this happy season was wrenched from us, because we Jews were identified with, of all things, that mystery cult, Christianity! I was marketing at the agora when the Roman soldier had come into our shop.

"You should have seen that pompous donkey!" Aquila shouted as he related the events of the afternoon. "He said that all Jews have to leave Rome."

"How can this be?" I demanded. "We are good Jews. And we are protected by law!"

Aquila raised an angry fist. "Emperor Claudius assumes that to be Jewish is to be Christian!" Tears of rage filled his darkened eyes.

"How short-sighted our emperor is!" I cried, knowing that there was nothing we could do but comply with the dreadful edict.

"But, Aquila, how can we? Our home is here. Our business. And all our friends." Tears of fear and frustration slipped from the corners of my eyes, making their way slowly in twin streams down to my quivering chin. *How can we live? Where can we go? What will happen to us?* My heart was overwhelmed with such questions. A sob broke free from my parched throat as I gave in to despair.

Aquila put his work-strengthened arms around me and gently pulled me to him. "There, there, Priscilla. Don't cry," he soothed. "Remember what the psalmist says, 'Whenever I am afraid, I will trust in you. In God (I will praise his words), In God I have put my trust; I will not fear. What can flesh do to me?'"[2]

His face brightened as he said, "I have a cousin in Corinth. I'll arrange everything. We'll go there, Priscilla!" He squeezed my hand. "Yes, we'll go to Corinth." He began to pace, as was his habit when excited or agitated. "We will set up our business in that great city. It's going to be all right, Priscilla." Aquila stopped pacing. He looked deeply into my tear-dimmed eyes and said, "It will be a new adventure!" *My dear Aquila, always the tender comforter and always the enterprising adventurer.*

I was busy sorting and packing when Aquila returned from the shop where he had purchased the latest maps for our move.

"We can't take that with us," Aquila said, pointing to the loom.

"Do we have to sell *everything?*" I cried in desperation. "This loom has always been in my family."

"Travel is so difficult," Aquila argued. "And the lighter we travel the better it will be." But my tears would not stop flowing. In the end, the loom was sold, as were most of our treasured belongings. Leaving had become more difficult because we were not only leaving our beloved home but most of the things that we loved, things that were so much a part of our lives. It was more difficult for me than it was for Aquila. Rome had always been my home; he was an adopted son of that glorious city. There is a saying that "all roads lead to Rome," but we were preparing to take one leading *out of* Rome. And sadly, all of our Jewish friends were faced with the same fearful plight.

It truly was an arduous journey, made more difficult because of our heavy hearts. We traveled for more than two months by land and by sea. We headed southeast by land to the Adriatic Sea. Milestones lined the Appian Way and ticked off the distance as we continued our weary journey. More than once we met a Roman soldier at one of the milestones, who compelled us to carry his load as well as our own to the next milestone. I guess you might say that that was the Roman way—on the Appian Way.

Aquila and I were side by side on our stouthearted donkeys when we were finally delighted by the first pungent aroma of the sea. It teased our senses as it embraced us with its leisurely southeastern breeze.

"Oh, Aquila," I said, leaning toward him. "Remember the psalmist's words? 'You have put all things under his feet, all sheep and oxen—even the beasts of the field, the birds of the air, and the fish of the sea that pass through the paths of the seas. O Lord, our Lord, how excellent is your name in all the earth!'[3] You were right, Aquila, this is an adventure! I pray that Yahweh will continue to guide and uphold us."

We spent the night at Tarentum and prayed for calm seas the next day. We were nearing the end of the "safe" period for sailing, between late spring and early autumn.[4]

As we made our way to the home of Jewish friends who had extended their hospitality to us, I said, "Oh, Aquila, I am so relieved that we will not have to stay at an inn."

"Oh, yes, my dear," he agreed. "We would not want to stay in any of the inns along the way because of the evil things that transpire within their gates."[5]

I was exhausted from the first part of our journey but found it difficult to sleep. After an eternity of tossing and turning, I saw the pale fingers of dawn paint the gray sky pink and lavender as the sun rose from the depths of the calm sea.

I looked forward to the last leg of the journey. We boarded the two-hundred-foot-long ship. It was carrying a cargo of grain to Corinth, the city of beauty, wealth, and corruption. *Well, we are big-city folks*, I mused. *We can handle it.*

The accommodations on the ship were nonexistent. We had to carry our own food aboard. Nothing was provided. In the evenings we stopped along the way, docking in one rough port after another. We had to find our own lodging at each stop.

On the third day out at sea, we were cautioned by the sailors to beware of an approaching vessel. "Take care," they warned. "It could be a pirate ship! That is not uncommon in these waters!"

We watched it approach, looming larger and more menacing by the moment. Aquila and I clung to one another, holding our breath. No one spoke as the apparition from the sea took on monstrous proportions as it grew ever nearer. Then, it was so close that we could make out the features of the sailors aboard the fearful vessel. What a relief when at last we became aware that the ship was another merchant vessel. It sailed by without incident. The rest of the trip was uneventful, however unpleasant it may have been.

At last! Corinth—that gem of the Roman Empire. The great city on the Corinthian Gulf where Greeks, Romans, Jews, and adventurers from the whole Mediterranean world gathered to transact business by day and (as we were to learn) patronize the night clubs by night. Thirty-three taverns composed the rear of the huge colonnade that was the largest nonreligious structure of ancient Greece. Corinth—a city of beauty and commerce, but also a city of corruption.

It was in the midst of all this that we established our business and our home. Of primary importance to us was the synagogue. We began making inquiries for the place of learning and worship. Providentially, Justus was one of the first people we met in Corinth. He quickly became one of our dearest friends.

In one of his more reflective moments, Justus reminded us of the terrible Exile our ancestors had suffered so long ago. He shook his head from side to side as Aquila and I agreed. "But," he said, "one of the great things it did for us was the establishment of the synagogue."

"You're right," Aquila said, "No matter where we are, we will find fellowship with other Jews." We found our fellowship in the synagogue that just happened to be next to Justus's home.

About a year after we settled in Corinth,[6] we had a visitor: Paul, a man rather small in size, bald-headed, bow-legged, with meeting eyebrows and a large, red, and somewhat hooked nose. But he was strongly built. He was full of grace, for at times he looked like a man, at times like an angel.[7]

"I, too, am a tentmaker," Paul told us. "I have heard about you, Aquila. Your reputation and craftsmanship are well known and attested."

"And yours as well, Paul," Aquila said. "We have heard that no one cuts a straighter line than does Paul of Tarsus."

Paul could not have come at a better time. Our business was growing. There was no doubt that we could use the help, so we spoke with him regarding a partnership. Our business relationship began the very next day.

The following Sabbath Paul joined us as we went to the synagogue. Come to think of it, it seems as though *he* led the way. I sat in the women's section, but I was never out of earshot. The resonance of Paul's words captured and kept captive my mind and soul.

His voice was not that of a great orator but was strong and confident as he began: "Shalom, dear friends," he said. "I deliver to you today a message that I brought to the people of Athens: I have Good News for you.

"You know that God made the world and everything in it. Since he created heaven and earth, it follows that he is Lord of heaven and earth. And, since he is Lord of all, he does not need to dwell in temples made with hands. No! Nor is he worshiped with human hands, as though he needed anything. It is he who gives to all life, breath, and all things. . . . So men and women should seek the Lord, in the earnest hope that they might grope for him and find him—though actually, he is not far from each and every one of us; for in him we live and move and have our being.[8]

"He now commands *all* men and women *everywhere* to repent. Do not be deceived. He has appointed a day on which he will judge the world in righteousness by the man Jesus, whom he has ordained. He has given assurance of this to all—by raising Jesus from the dead.[9]

"Brothers and sisters, the long-awaited Messiah has come. He is our Lord and Savior, Jesus Christ—the Resurrection and the Life!"

Have you ever had such a thrill of excitement that you seemed to be able to physically feel it, from the inside out? Did you ever have a sudden realization that a truth you had longed for over an endless period of time was at last made known? Did that realization block out all other sights and sounds around you? That is exactly what I experienced as I heard Paul speak of the Messiah. I was breathless with an exhilaration of being more alive than I had ever been before! What caused such stirring in my soul? *I know!* my enraptured heart cried. *It is joy!*

I could hardly wait to talk with Aquila and with Paul. *Had Aquila experienced the same quickening in his spirit? Would Paul tell us more?* I was so eager to hear more of this Good News that I could think of nothing else.

At last Paul, Aquila and I took leave of our friends with a fond farewell and shalom. We made our way down the quiet Corinthian street, evening having advanced to darkening night. The excitement grew within me, yet I could find no words to express my newfound joy. When we were finally home and seated on our cushions, I found six words, "Paul, tell me about the Messiah." Aquila pulled his cushion closer to Paul. *He is as intent on Paul's words as I.*

"All my life I have studied the Scriptures," Paul said. "I am a Pharisee of Pharisees. I have studied under the greatest rabbi in all of Israel. I was a chief persecutor of the Christian sect called 'The Way.' Then, on my way to Damascus, I had an unexpected visitor." He paused, searching for just the right words to describe what occurred on that dusty road.

He became a word sculptor, crafting each phrase to clearly and thoughtfully define the extraordinary meeting between him and the Risen Savior. "I had the high priest's letters with me," he began. "I was on a mission to deliver them to the priests in Damascus. The high priest was grateful for my willingness to help in the fight against this 'dangerous cult,' as he put it. I agreed with his assessment of The Way, and was happy to bring the letters to Damascus. My intention was to round up all the Christians and bring them back to Jerusalem—in chains." Tears of remorse blurred his vision.

"Ah," he continued, blinking back the flow that threatened to course its way down his weathered cheeks. "But God is gracious, slow to condemn, and quick to forgive. He met me on that road, before I could reach my destination." His eyes shone with renewed brightness. "It was right there, on that thoroughfare that I had an encounter—with God!"

"What happened, Paul?" I whispered with bated breath.

Aquila's eyes and mine locked in a moment of profound expectancy. Then, Paul told us what occurred. "My companions and I had almost reached Damascus. We could see the city, looming before us." Aquila and I leaned forward, not wanting to miss a single word.

"Suddenly a brilliant light flashed from the sky," Paul continued, moving his arm in a wide arc to demonstrate the vastness of the light that had encompassed him. "It overwhelmed me! I closed my eyes to shield them from its fearful radiance. I fell to the ground as though struck by some awesome force. Even as I fell, I heard a voice speaking my name, 'Saul, Saul.' Then the voice said, 'Why are you persecuting me?' I responded with a question of my own: 'Tell me, Lord, who are you?' The voice's answer was unmistakable, 'I am Jesus,' he said, 'whom you are persecuting.'"

Paul rose from his cushion then, and began pacing the floor in the passion of the memory. "That was the beginning," he said. "Jesus told me to rise and to go to Damascus, and that I would be told what to do next. I rose from the ground. My companions had seen the light but had not heard Jesus' voice. As I brushed the dust from my tunic I opened my eyes. *I could not see!* I blinked. Still no vision. It was darker than night. I was blind! My companions led me by the hand to the Street called Straight. The blindness lasted three days during which I took no food or drink. My sight was not restored until Ananias came to see me.

"That disciple of Jesus laid his hands on me and said, 'Saul, my brother, the Lord Jesus, who appeared to you on your way here, has sent me to you so that you may recover your sight and be filled with the Holy Spirit.' Immediately, my dear friends, the scales were lifted from my eyes and I could see! I praised God and was baptized. Jesus, whom I had been persecuting, became my salvation! I have preached his Good News ever since!"[10]

I felt a thrill of hope as Paul reminded us of the promises in the Scriptures and of the way Yahweh had told our people through the prophets that he would send a Redeemer. Paul read the passages that described the Savior. And the description was that of Jesus of Nazareth!

"Christ died for our sins according to the Scriptures, and he was buried, and he rose again the third day according to the Scriptures. . . . Therefore, from now on, we regard no one according to the flesh. Even though we have known Christ according to the flesh, yet now we know him thus no longer. Therefore, if anyone is in Christ, he is a new creation; old things have passed away; behold all things have become new."[11]

The old things have passed away. *I am* a new creation. Life took on new meaning for Aquila and me then. Even our business took on new life. We used every opportunity to learn more about the Messiah. And we were driven to share what we learned with everyone who would listen.

But then, that evil day came. The day when the opposition in the synagogue grew so blasphemous that Paul's anger rose. His voice rang with fervor as he said to his adversaries, "Your blood be upon your own heads; I am clean of your clear rejection of Scriptures. From this moment on I will bring the Good News of redemption to the Gentiles."

And so he did, taking my husband and me with him. Aquila and I had always been good Jews, proud to be God's chosen people. A new realization of *why* we were chosen became clear to us as we opened our home for worship and study—the worship and study of Jesus, the Messiah. It was a glorious time of spiritual growth. I thank the Lord God for those precious times, for it became clear that God was preparing us for our next adventure, travel to another distant city, across another unfamiliar sea.

In the year A.D. **52,** we sailed with Paul. Our attachment to Corinth was not the same as it was to Rome, so when Paul said, "It is time for me to preach the Good News in Antioch," we were eager to accompany him. We agreed with his decision to leave Corinth, as hostility was growing against our dear brother in Christ. He had his hair cut off in Cenchreae, the Corinthian port from which we sailed. "I have taken a vow," was his only explanation.

The Aegean Sea was beautiful that time of year and although Paul seemed preoccupied, Aquila and I enjoyed the view of the numerous Greek isles we passed along the way. "This trip has been far more pleasant than the one from Rome," I told Aquila as we gazed at the calm waters of the blue-green sea.

"Yes," he agreed. "But we are on our way to another pagan city, almost as large, I understand, as Corinth. I have heard that there is a theater in Ephesus that seats twenty-five thousand persons."

"Well," I suggested, "they must be a cultured people."

"We shall see," was his only response.

At last the great port city came into view. The first thing I noticed was the towering gate west of the dock. "Look," I said, pointing to the massive structure. "I have never seen so impressive an entrance into a city. Even Rome does not boast such a wonder!"

"Wonder!" Aquila said. "Wait until you see one of the seven wonders of the world, right here in Ephesus!"

"What could that be?" I asked.

"Remember, we are in Greece," he said. "That 'wonder' is the pagan Temple of Diana. I have heard that the edifice is supported by no less than one hundred and twenty-seven columns. Such pride is there in this idolatrous goddess that the people of this city have even minted a coin in her honor."

I was horrified at such deification. There was much work to be done in this, the most important trade center west of Tarsus. "Of all the myriad people living here," I wondered aloud, "how many are followers of The Way?"

Paul had joined us by that time and he responded as I knew he would. "We are here, dear friends, to enlighten the Ephesians in The Way, to assure them that Christ is risen and that salvation is for all who will receive him. First, to the synagogue," he said, leading the way off the ship. That's how Paul was, a great man of action! Before Aquila and I had gathered our belongings, Paul had begun his hurried search for the synagogue.

Finally it was Aquila's and my turn to make our way through the majestic gate and down the wide main thoroughfare. A succession of enormous columns lined both sides of the foremost road of the city. Behind the columns were rows of elegantly designed buildings, baths, and gymnasiums. The spacious avenue led straight to the magnificent theater. From there we could see the Temple of Diana, towering above the bustling city. Aquila asked for directions to the synagogue, and before long, we found ourselves on a narrow street, some distance from the dock from which we had come.

We shook the dust from our sandals and entered the humble edifice that was the meeting place for the Ephesian Jews, their beloved synagogue. It was no surprise to find Paul in the midst of a debate. "I tell you, my friends," he was saying as we entered the darkened building, "the Messiah has come! He is Jesus of Nazareth. All Holy Scripture points to him, and he has fulfilled the prophecies that were spoken of him." He began to outline the prophetic Scriptures, but got no further than Micah's words that the Messiah would come from Bethlehem, the birthplace of our Savior.

"Paul," the oldest man of the group broke in, "who are you, to come into our midst and preach such profanity? Jesus, the Son of God? What blasphemy!"

Paul continued the debate for several more minutes, but his words fell on the hard soil of hearts darkened, perhaps, by their pagan community. He turned on his heel and left the knot of dissenters to join us at the rear of the synagogue.

"Your work here will not be easy, my friends," he told us. "But I know that with God's help you will persevere and lead people to the truth of the Messiah."

"Won't you stay?" we asked.

"No, I must keep the feast in Jerusalem before continuing my work among the Gentiles." We embraced amid our tears, and then our friend and mentor was gone.

"What will we do?" I asked Aquila. "Here we are in a strange city, with no friends and a mission for the Lord."

"But we do have friends," he assured me. "And we will make more as we establish our business here, just as we did in Corinth."

Of course Aquila was right, and in no time, it seemed, we had established God's church in our home. The meetings were filled with love and passion as we shared the wonderful news of redemption. Our church had a fine mix of men and women, Jews and Gentiles. Our worship was pure joy and delight in the Lord. We spent every Lord's Day together, breaking bread, singing psalms of praise, and sharing the teaching of our Lord and Savior, Jesus the Messiah. New converts were added every day.

"How good of the Lord to provide such a lovely and large home," Aquila noted as we prepared for our Lord's Day meeting.

"Yes," I agreed. "But pray for fine weather. The courtyard is our most spacious room. As our numbers have grown, we will have to meet there, beneath the sky."

"We'll erect a canopy," Aquila suggested.

With that, the first worshipers arrived, accompanied by someone I did not recognize. Aquila and I joined our friends and introduced ourselves to the newcomer.

"Shalom, friend," Aquila said, smiling warmly. "I am Aquila and this is my wife, Priscilla."

"Shalom to you, dear friends in Christ," he said. "I am Apollos. I have just arrived from Alexandria in Egypt."

Joy filled my soul at the sound of his name. "Ah, Apollos," I said. "Your name is not unknown to us. We have heard of your eloquent preaching."

Nor was Alexandria unknown to me. It was in that great city of learning and culture that our Scriptures were translated into the Greek language, making them more accessible since most Jews spoke Greek. And it was clear that Apollos was well versed in the Word of God.

Followers of our Lord kept arriving. At last worship began. I opened the meeting with prayer. "I will praise you, O Lord, among the peoples; I will sing to you among the nations. For your mercy reaches unto the heavens, and your truth unto the clouds. Be exalted, O God, above the heavens; let your glory be above all the earth."[12]

We asked Apollos to share his testimony. He had a silver tongue and charismatic manner.

"Be baptized and repent," he began. "The kingdom of God is at hand! Forgiveness is for those who truly repent and turn from their sinful ways. Live a life that demonstrates that repentance. If you have two coats, give one to the poor. If you have food, share it with the hungry."[13]

He continued in this vein for nearly an hour. Then he looked toward heaven and prayed: "Have mercy upon me, O God, according to your lovingkindness . . . blot out my transgressions. Wash me thoroughly from my iniquity, and cleanse me from my sin. . . . Create in me a clean heart, O God, and renew a steadfast spirit within me. . . . A broken and a contrite heart—these, O God, you will not despise."[14]

All too soon the meeting was over and our friends in the Lord rose to leave. Aquila called to them as they made their way through our outer gate. "We'll meet again tomorrow, at the synagogue."

The buzz of overlapping conversations was replaced by the silence of the evening as Aquila and I helped our servants tidy up. At last my husband and I were alone.

"Aquila," I began, "Apollos is such a dear brother, and his preaching so clear. But, I am troubled."

"I know," my husband agreed. "Something seemed missing in his teaching. Let us encourage him to speak at synagogue tomorrow. Perhaps then we will hear his teaching of God's grace."

As planned, we met our Christian friends at the synagogue the next evening. We arrived to find Apollos surrounded by admiring and questioning men and women. We had no difficulty persuading him to preach to his eager admirers. We watched as his spellbinding words enthralled the congregation. He was magnificent. But he was only giving half the message. Just as he had done the day before, he was calling for repentance in the manner of John the Baptist, but he was not telling the complete story. Missing from Apollos's teaching were the great truths of redemption and eternal life.

"Come home with us, Apollos," I suggested after the worship meeting. "Aquila and I would like to talk with you, if we may."

Apollos was as gracious as he was eloquent. He joined us. He listened—with profound appreciation.

"How wonderful! How glorious!" he exclaimed. "We can look to Jesus, the author and finisher of our faith, who for the joy that was set before him endured the cross, despising the shame, and now—*and now*—has sat down at the right hand of the throne of God."[15]

Our dear friend Apollos went on to be a great leader of the church in Corinth.

Apollos left Ephesus. Paul returned, more on fire for the Lord than ever. For three months he spoke in his own bold manner, reasoning and persuading concerning the things of the kingdom of God.

"Perhaps we need to be more careful," Aquila cautioned our friend. "There is a growing hardness in some hearts."

"Oh, yes, Paul." I added, "I have even heard evil, horrid things spoken about Jesus and The Way."

Undaunted, Paul said, "Come then, let us go to the school of

Tyrannus. We will hold our meetings there. We will not be silent regarding our Lord and Savior!"—as if our dear brother could ever be silent about anything on his heart, especially those things concerning Jesus.

As might be suspected, enemies were always on hand, ready to strike. We were nearly killed in the silversmith's riot that rocked the city. Being a businesswoman myself, I understood their concern about the tradesmen's declining sales. But, being a Christian, I stood beside Paul in his arguments against buying those scurrilous silver idols.

One of the silversmiths spoke forcefully to the assembled craftsmen. "This Paul has persuaded many people and turned them away, saying that these works of ours are not gods at all, simply because we made them with our hands, *skillful* hands! Furthermore, not only is this trade of ours in danger of falling into disrepute, but also the temple of the great goddess Diana. It may become despised because of his words, and Diana's magnificence destroyed—Diana, whom all Asia and the world worship."

The silversmith's address turned the mob ugly. You could *feel* their hot, growling anger. It was a groundswell, reminiscent of an earthquake. They shouted through clenched teeth, "Great is Diana of the Ephesians!"

Before we knew it, the whole city was filled with confusion. Great hoards of people rushed into the theater with one accord, like a mighty, swollen river rushing downstream. They seized Paul's traveling companions, Gaius and Aristarchus.

"Hurry!" Aquila shouted to Simon, one of our companions. "Go! Find the city clerk! We need his help to quiet this mob."

Simon set off immediately, pushing his way through the crowd and disappearing into the sea of humanity.

Paul shouted above the noise of the crazed mob. "I'm going into the theater."

"No, you must not! You cannot go in there!" I insisted.

"It would be suicide!" Aquila added.

At that very moment, the officials we had sent for arrived. They were friends of Paul's as well. Thank God Paul listened to their warnings and did not enter the theater.

Then the Lord (the God of miracles) did a miraculous thing. He caused the people in the theater to become confused. By this time, most of them did not even know why they were there! There was some further discussion, and once or twice it looked as though the riot would break out again, but the city clerk quieted the crowd. He told them to bring their charges to court, adding, "We are in danger of being charged with rioting for today's uproar, because there is no valid reason that we can give for this disorderly gathering. If Rome demands an explanation, we will not know what to say."

When the assembly finally dispersed, we drew a collective sigh of relief![16]

Immediately following the riot, Paul prepared to go to Macedonia. How sad we all were to see our brother in Christ depart. We prayed long and fervently for his safety and for the growth of the church, just as he asked.

Some time later that year we heard the startling news. It spread like wildfire. Emperor Claudius had died.

"What will happen now?" I demanded of Aquila.

"I'm not sure, Prisca," he replied. "But I've heard rumors that the edict that expelled us from Rome may be lifted." Tears of joy filled my eyes as he added, "Maybe—just maybe, we can go home."

Home! To see the seven hills of Rome! To walk the wide avenues. To be in familiar surroundings that I had known and loved since childhood. God prepared the way—and as soon as the edict was officially lifted, my dear Aquila and I went home.

Home, where we worked with other Christians in the church, spreading the Good News of redemption. Although we maintained our business in Ephesus, we were now free to travel and spend time in both cities. God greatly enlarged our ministry, and we have been busy ever since.

How ironic: while we were in Ephesus, Paul was in prison in Rome. Timothy shared Paul's letter with us. It reminded us of the letter he had written to the Christians in Rome.

We read that letter over and over again, memorizing his words. How precious are his closing thoughts, cherished by Christians everywhere: "May the grace of our Lord Jesus Christ be with you all. I commit you to God, who is able to make you strong and steady in the Lord, just as the Gospel says. And just as I have told you.

"This is God's plan of salvation for you—kept secret from the beginning of time. But now, as the prophets foretold, and as God commands, this message is being preached everywhere, so that people all around the world will have faith in Christ and obey him.

"To God, who alone is wise, be the glory forever—through Jesus Christ our Lord. Amen."[17]

NOTES

1. The early Roman religious system was known as Penates.

2. Psalm 56:3,4, New King James Version

3. Psalm 8:6b–9, New King James Version

4. May twenty-sixth and September fourteenth.

5. Inns were dangerous places, and also dens of iniquity that provided prostitutes for travelers.

6. Around A.D. 50.

7. Onesiphorus wrote this description of Paul in "Acts of Paul and Thecla."

8. Acts 17:24–28, paraphrased

9. Acts 17:31, paraphrased

10. Acts 9:1–19, paraphrased

11. 1 Corinthians 15:34, 2 Corinthians 5:16,17, New King James Version

12. Psalm 57:9–11, New King James Version

13. Luke 3:3,8,11, paraphrased

14. Psalm 51:1–2,10,17b, New King James Version

15. Hebrews 12:2, New King James Version

16. Acts 19:22–41, paraphrased

17. Romans 16:24–27, paraphrased